to Lee
 with warmest regards —
 Pat
 Dec. 9, 2011

PADUCAH'S '37 FLOOD
RIVERGEES

PADUCAH'S '37 FLOOD
RIVERGEES

by
Pat Taylor

13-digit International Standard Book Number   978-0-9758788-5-9
Library of Congress Card Catalog Number   2010940523

Cover design and book layout by Asher Graphics
Edited by Carol Asher

Manufactured in the United States of America

All book order correspondence should be addressed to:

Sweetbriar Books
4570 Westchester Lane
Paducah, KY 42003

270-534-0088
www.rivergees.com
pat.taylor@rivergees.com

...Dorothy, remembering her manners, said, "We'll never be able to thank you enough for taking in this bunch of refugees."

Nick said heartily, "You ain't refugees, you're family and you'd do the same for us. Have another biscuit."

"What's rivergees?" three-year-old Nell asked.

The location of the cover photograph was 4th and Washington Street.
It shows the Washington Street side of the home and office of
Dr. Samuel B. Pulliam at 312 South 4th Street. It is the present location of the
Paducah Water Works office.

This book is dedicated to my husband Jim, with love and thanks for his patience, support and enthusiasm for this effort.

for our children
Brian, Kathy, Nick, Holly, and Brad

and our grandchildren
Valerie, Emmy, Ty, Abby, and Dalton

With special thanks to Mary Warren, ("Pudge")
for her invaluable contribution.

And to Brad Nelson, for his computer expertise.

In loving memory of my parents, H. B. and Louise Hargrove

CHAPTER

 1

In December of 1936, the little river city of Paducah, Kentucky was struggling through the seventh year of the Great Depression. Money was scarce, jobs were jealously guarded and celebrating Christmas was a challenge. H.B. Hargrove, Jr. supported his family by working as a lobby artist at the Columbia Amusement Company, a group of movie theaters owned by Leo Keiler. The hours were long and pay was short but it somehow put food on the table and paid the rent for his family's half of a little gray duplex at the corner of 4th and Adams Street.

Like almost all wives and mothers of that time, Louise stayed at home and kept house. She was kept busy taking care of their toddler Patsy, cleaning, cooking and sewing. She took pride in the three small rooms and prized a new dining room suite that was being bought "on time," and a walnut secretary that gave dignity to the living room. The landlady, Mrs. Harrigan, had agreed to new wallpaper when they moved in and Louise had made it a pleasant home.

That year it took an effort to bring some cheer to the season. Louise's mother, Sallie Dalton, had died of pneumonia in February of that year and her grief was still fresh. But a small Christmas tree sporting a string of colored lights and a few small ornaments stood in the living room and Santa Claus had left a baby doll and doll buggy under the tree for two-year-old Patsy.

Christmas Day was unseasonably mild and clear. Windows

and doors stood open as Patsy pushed her new doll buggy up and down the sidewalk in front of the house. Christmas carols rang from the radio and neighbors stood out on their porches and in their yards wishing each other a Merry Christmas and enjoying the beautiful day.

Even in those hard times—and maybe in a way because of them—families gathered to celebrate Christmas Day and each other. At midday H.B. and Louise, pushing Patsy in her stroller, walked to H.B.'s parents' dark little house on South 9th Street. His sister Louise lived in Louisville with her husband J. B. McNeely and their three-year-old son, Jimmy. Pretty, lively Mary Lee and handsome seventeen-year-old Dick still lived at home with their parents. Mary Lee worked as a sales clerk at List's Drug Store. Dick would graduate from Augusta Tilghman High School the following spring.

Mary Lee happily met them at the door, delighted with the cookies and fudge that Louise had made for them. "Oh, golly—two kinds of fudge! You're the Tops, Louise. Get away from it, Dick. I saw it first." With her dark hair and eyes, she resembled H.B. but in place of his serious, responsible demeanor, Mary Lee was vivacious and fun-loving and she was to be Patsy's favorite aunt and lifelong friend.

The women folk gathered in the crowded kitchen, getting in each other's way. Mary Lee and Louise trotted back and forth setting the table. Horace appeared at the kitchen door, rubbing his hands together.

"Can you do anything for me, Bess?" he asked, affecting a beggar's whine. Bess flapped a dish towel at him and said, "Shoo!" They all laughed at the familiar routine.

Horace asked the blessing over Bess's incomparable chicken and dressing. Bowls of home-canned vegetables and plates of hot biscuits went around the table amidst a babble of happy conversation…."this dressing is larrupin"…"What did ol' Santa Claus bring you, Patsy?"…"Mama, you make the best biscuits"…"pass the string beans, please"…"any more blackberry preserves?"…"wonder what the McNeelys are doing…wish they were here."

Gifts were small, modest and practical, mostly homemade, and were given with love and received with pleasure and real appreciation. For one blessed day, hard times were forgotten in the closeness of family.

Later in the afternoon, bearing more cookies and fudge, they rode the Noble Park bus out to 19th and Park Avenue, walking the rest of the way to Louise's father's house at 1762 Madison Street where he lived with Louise's unmarried sister, Dorothy. The extended family, including Louise's brother Frank and his wife, Ondine, and her brother Ralph and his wife, Nannette, and nine-year-old daughter, Mary Warren, whom Patsy adored, gathered for Christmas supper.

Harry Dalton was quiet and subdued, remembering that last Christmas his wife of forty-four years had been at his side. However, he was comforted by the presence of his family. He was a tailor like his father and grandfather before him and had a shop at 117 South 4th Street. His eldest son, Harry, lived with his wife, Matt, and their three sons, Jack, Billy and Bobby in faraway New York City. Ondine and Frank had no children.

"How's business, Ralph?" inquired Frank.

Only a month before, Ralph had gone heavily into debt to build and equip a new dry-cleaning plant on North 13th Street. He and Nannette had been working long hours to get it going and business was beginning to come in, giving them reason to hope for some measure of success. "Pretty slow, but startin' to come in," Ralph replied.

Frank worked as a caller at the Illinois Central Railroad Shops and half envied, half pitied Ralph for the risk he had taken in those difficult times.

Patsy Hargrove

Brown eyes shining, Mary Warren said, "Tell about the telephone, Daddy."

"Oh—yeah—we've had a telephone put in. You can't run a business without one."

"Tell the phone number, Daddy. It's 1-2-9," she sang, unable to wait for her father to reply, "and when you answer it, you don't say 'hello,' you say 'Dalton Cleaners'."

Dinner over, plates of Louise's cookies and fudge were passed around the table. "Good candy, Sis," Frank commented. "What kind is it?"

Louise was pleased. "That's Mexican Orange Fudge. You've had it before. It's Mom's recipe...she made it every Christmas"... her voice caught. Everyone grew quiet as sadness descended over the table.

Nannette broke the silence. "Why don't we go see what's under the Christmas tree?"

As the youngest-but-one, Mary Warren was allowed to distribute the gifts. They were opened to exclamations of surprise and pleasure and soon the floor was littered with tissue and scraps of ribbon.

Patsy basked in Mary Warren's attention as she played tirelessly with the toddler, carried her around like a doll and called her "Princess Pat." Mary Warren's nickname within the family was "Pudgie"— an odd nickname for a tall, slender child. The grown-ups' conversation flowed over and around them. Patsy fell asleep on the living room floor and the thirty-sixth Christmas of the twentieth century came to a close.

H.B. Hargrove

Louise Hargrove

CHAPTER

2

On Sunday, December 27, H.B. and Louise woke to heavy clouds and cold. While Louise made breakfast, H.B. went out to the coal shed and filled a coal bucket. He chopped some kindling wood and made his way back into the house, feeling the sting of sleet against his face. When Patsy woke up, Louise dressed her warmly and settled her in her high-chair. She began to spoon oatmeal into an uninterested little mouth while H.B. stoked the coal stove that heated their house.

The wind rose and sleet began falling thick and fast. Louise let Patsy down to play and when H.B. had finished his breakfast she began to clear away the breakfast dishes. She heated a kettle of water on the gas stove and brought in a metal dishpan from its hook on the back porch, shook in some soap powder and tilted the kettle into it, steam rising above it. Some houses were now equipped with hot water heaters, but they were not yet considered essential. What you've never had, you don't miss.

Even though it was Sunday, H.B. left the house to go to his sign shop in the Arcade Theatre building. The concept of a five-day workweek, or an eight-hour day, was meaningless in those times. He was grateful to have the job and grateful, too, that new signs were constantly needed as the movie bill changed frequently and new signs advertising coming films had to be provided quickly for three theatres: the Arcade, the elegant Columbia and the Little, later to be known as the Rialto. Current movies were shown on Sunday and Monday, the bill changing for more important movies on Tuesday, Wednesday and Thursday. Friday and Saturday were reserved mainly for "B" movies, with a serial, sometimes a western, sometimes science-fiction, and sometimes a mystery on Saturday afternoon.

He walked briskly through the quiet neighborhood, facing a north wind. Except for a couple of brick apartment buildings, the houses along South 4th Street were mainly modest frame dwellings, most of them built around the turn of the century, a few long before. Most of the houses were neatly kept, porches and sidewalks swept, windows washed.

One house had stood unpainted for many years, its roof in the last stages of disrepair. Even before the hard years of Depression, the neighbors had complained that if it were painted now the weight of the paint would probably pull it down. H.B. smiled to himself as he remembered an expression that excused neglect— "Too poor to paint and too proud to whitewash."

A couple of Plymouth Rock hens pecked dejectedly in the yard next door and a woman emerged from the house, her hair tightly wound in metal rollers. Flapping an apron at them, she chased them into the back yard enclosure.

St. Paul Lutheran Church stood between Clark and Adams Street and now the door opened and the sexton appeared at the door as he prepared the old church for Sunday services.

H.B. turned west on Broadway. The business district was deserted and his footsteps echoed hollowly in the cold air. Ragged Christmas garlands still stretched from one side of the street to the other. Several business places were abandoned and boarded up, debris collecting at the entrances, victims of the Depression.

The theatre would open for the matinee at one o'clock, but for now the building was silent. On a weekday morning the arcade would be astir with the several businesses housed in it. He noticed that a new shop, The Pin Money Frock Shop, advertising ladies' dresses and smocks for a dollar each, was being prepared for a grand opening on the 9th of January. It was heartening to see that some-

14

one had courage enough to take that risk. Maybe it was a sign that the grip of the depression was easing a little, he hoped.

He walked through the arcade toward the theatre lobby, turned to the right down a short hallway, then turned left to enter the cramped sign shop, pulling the string on the overhead light. The sign advertising the movie that had just closed stood waiting for him. The large signs were made on 4 x 8 foot Upson boards that were purchased from Iseman Lumber Company on South 4th Street.

Checking his supplies, he saw that he would need to mix more paint to cover the lettering and artwork on the board. He removed some 8 x 10-inch black-and-white glossies that he had thumb-tacked to the sign and put them in a file cabinet, at the same time removing the yellow envelope that held the stills for the next movie. It was to be a comedy and would play on New Year's Eve. The sign would have to be painted over, and he felt a familiar pang of regret that the artwork he had so painstakingly applied would be gone forever. Assembling a portfolio, he tried to make a snapshot of each sign before it gave way to the next one.

H.B.'s movie signs.

He pulled on an old pair of paint-spattered overalls and shoes, rolled up his sleeves and started to work.

Finding a bucket, he opened a new 5 pound box of Tamms' Kalsomine Powder, scooped out a cupful and mixed it with tap water to a creamy consistency. He chose a light blue to cover the buff he had used previously. He was getting low on li   reen. He laid the

H.B.'s movie signs.

board on the floor and started painting over it with a wide brush, setting his jaw as he painted over the lifelike depiction of Claudette Colbert. The distinctive odor of the paint blended with the smell of paint thinner pleasantly.

Posters and show cards of movies of the past were tacked to the walls of the shop. An assortment of poster paints stood in a wheeled trolley near a large easel and his paint brushes stood in a jar of paint thinner. A nondescript cabinet with grooved shelves, once used to hold the wax recordings that provided the soundtrack for the earliest days of sound film, stood against the wall. Now it held a few art instruction books and some back issues of *Signs of the Times* magazine. A high paint-speckled stool stood beside the easel.

H.B. didn't mind the quiet, but would like someday to be able to buy a small radio for the shop. He loved good music. He would like to save some money to buy a phonograph, too. Who knew when that would be, with money so tight and more essential needs pressing every day. There were still several months left to pay for the dining room suite, and he knew that Louise would like to have a telephone.

Telephones were still considered a luxury, though. The

Clarks, who lived in the other side of the duplex, had a telephone, as it was necessary for Otto's work. They were always good about letting them use the telephone when necessary and Louise could order a week's supply of groceries or a month's supply of coal from it. Louise was a good manager and could stretch his meager paycheck a long way and still put satisfying meals on the table. He thought about Louise and Patsy now, wishing he were at home.

H.B.'s movie signs.

It was chilly in the

shop. He wondered about the weather. The forecast had not been encouraging. Glancing at the clock he kept on a nearby shelf he noticed that it had stopped.

A sound from the hallway told him that Molly Vance, the cleaning woman, had come in from the empty theatre and was putting away her mop and pail. He liked Mrs. Vance. She was an elderly Irish woman who worked hard to provide for herself and her invalid husband and often had a kind word of inquiry about Louise and Patsy. Having no children of her own, she took a lively interest in the little girl.

In a moment her gray head poked around the door. "It's a terrible day to be out and about. The weather's somethin' fierce."

"Hello, Mrs. Vance," he replied. "It was plenty bad when I came in, and I reckon it's gonna get worse. You wouldn't happen to know what time it is, would you?"

Shaking her head, she turned back to the task at hand. "Here's Will now. Maybe he knows."

Will Blanks, a porter at the theatres, greeted them pleasantly and said that he had come in at ten o'clock.

H.B. finished painting over the sign board and set it upright to dry. He cleaned his paint brush, then, taking out some poster board, he measured off several pieces for show cards and began cutting

H.B.'s movie signs.

H.B.'s movie signs.

them out with a pair of large shears. He had an unconscious habit of moving his jaws in rhythm with the shears as he cut.

Placing one of the cards on the big easel, he consulted the list of movies to be advertised over the next few weeks. These cards would contain only the titles of the movies and the names of the stars in an appropriate lettering style, sometimes accented with glitter to draw the eye to them. They would be displayed inside glass cases placed strategically along the walls of the arcade and in the lobbies of the theatres.

First, he measured the spacing for the lettering; then, with a sharp pencil, he lightly sketched off the title of a Sonja Heine movie and stirred the yellow paint in one of the cans on the trolley. He dipped a brush into it and, steadying his right hand by holding the back of his left hand under his right wrist, he executed a graceful "S" on the blue posterboard. When the card was finished, but while the paint was still wet, he shook gold glitter over the title and propped it up. Any traces of pencil markings that remained would be removed with an art-gum eraser.

He finished several cards, then went to the file cabinet and pulled out the promotional material for the next attraction. This would suggest the idea for the artwork on the big sign and he would line it off to scale, multiplying the scale several times for the large area to be covered.

He suddenly realized that he was hungry. *It must be about lunchtime*, he thought. He changed to his street clothes, put on his coat and hat and emerged from the shop, dreading to go outside. The weather had not improved.

He started for home, but as he passed the White Owl Diner he decided to stop and eat a quick lunch, then go straight back to work.

Mounting two steps, he pushed through the door. A wave of warmth engulfed him. Cigarette smoke hung on the air, mingled with an appetizing aroma from the grill. Several customers were being served amidst a friendly clatter.

The little diner was known for its barbecue and its remarkably good hamburgers. Those hamburgers were five cents apiece and twenty-five cents would buy a half-dozen.

He sat down at the counter and ordered a hamburger and a cup of coffee. The hamburger was hot off the grill, served with thinly sliced onion and dill pickle on a fresh warm bun with a handful of crisp potato chips on the side. He stirred cream and two spoonsful of sugar into the steaming, fragrant coffee. It was a good lunch and well worth the ten cents it cost.

As he started back to the theatre, he pulled his coat collar up and hunched his shoulders against the cold. It was getting worse. Freezing rain now mingled with the sleet and icy patches were forming on the sidewalk. At 4th and Broadway he looked across the street at the big clock on the corner of the Citizen's Bank Building, locally known as the "Ten Story Building." It was 12:25. Five more minutes would put him back in the shop, so he would wind the clock and set it for 12:30.

The theatre was coming to life now. The ushers had appeared and were changing into their brass-buttoned, maroon and gray uniforms and Miss Hattie was getting ready to take her place at the ticket window. Mr. Butler was already in the projection room, arranging the reels for the short subject and trailers. For twenty-

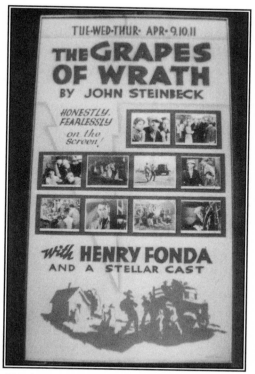

H.B.'s movie signs.

seven cents (eleven cents for children), movie patrons could enjoy the feature film, a short subject and/or cartoon, a newsreel, and previews of coming attractions. The same program at the Columbia would cost forty cents for an adult ticket, fifteen cents for a child.

The afternoon's work proceeded uneventfully. The year was drawing to a close and soon the Arcade's Christmas decorations would be brought in to be stored away until next year. His thoughts turned to his plans for a sign advertising a movie for New Year's Eve. There was always a midnight movie for the occasion and the crowd could become rowdy. Even though he could get passes to see the movie he and Louise would be glad to stay quietly at home.

He worked steadily, aware of the muffled sound of moviegoers chatting their way through the lobby, joking with the doorman.

From time to time a burst of laughter greeted some bit of folly on the big screen. Suddenly the lights flickered, went out… flickered again…came back on…flickered out. It was pitch dark in the shop. Feeling his way past the easel he tried to cover the open paint cans before the paint could begin to thicken, groped for a rag to wipe his brush and put the brush in what he hoped was the jar of paint thinner.

The sound of rhythmic clapping and a shrill whistle could be heard from the theatre in protest at the interrupted entertainment. He remembered an usher's flashlight in a drawer in the file cabinet and used it to find his way to the hallway. By that time, it was apparent that the lights were off to stay.

Disgruntled movie patrons were leaving. Miss Hattie was flustered. "No, I can't give you no money back. Come on back tomorrow and tell 'em in the office."

H.B. knew his day's work was over. He reached for his coat and hat, disappointed at having to leave his work unfinished but relieved to be on his way home. When he reached the sidewalk he saw that the power lines were coated with ice and the weight of the ice had pulled down the lines at the intersection of 5th and Broadway.

He walked the block and a half to 4th and Broadway to turn south toward home and family. He crossed Kentucky Avenue, passed by the old red-brick City Hall and walked quickly up South 4th Street. Several large ice-crusted branches had broken and blocked a part of the sidewalk and street.

He reflected that it was a good thing that Louise had made a trip to the grocery store yesterday instead of waiting to phone in an order on Monday. Mr. Meacham's delivery boy might not be able to make it in the delivery truck if the streets stayed this slick. Milk would be delivered from a horse-drawn wagon, the bottles left on the front porch before daylight.

Every year the old-fashioned delivery wagons were fewer, and H.B. missed them. Trash was still collected in the alley behind the house in a disreputable looking wagon pulled by an evil-tempered mule; a silent black man drove a salvage wagon with rubber tires on its wheels. Plenty of farm wagons were still to be seen on summer Saturdays at the Market House.

He remembered a produce wagon that belonged to the Nickias family, one of several Greek families who lived in Paducah. When H.B. was a boy, Mr. Nickias drove the wagon laden with fruits and vegetables in season during the warm months. His bashful little daughter was often with him, long black braids swinging on either side of her sallow little face.

Besides the fresh produce, Mr. Nickias's wagon featured a jar of candy colored a bright pink. At the rear, a covered pot hung from a frame under which an oil flame burned. Popcorn was poured into the pot, covered, and heated until at last little muffled explosions gave evidence of popping corn which would be scooped out into bags and sold for a penny or two.

After nightfall, when Mr. Nickias headed for home, only the light from the oil burner could still be seen in the darkness, swinging spookily from side to side with the motion of the wagon. The little daughter, braids now wound around her head, was grown and married to Gus Kappas and Mr. Nickias still drove the fruit wagon, minus the popcorn and candy.

And now he was home. It was only 3:30. As he opened the door he whistled two notes. From the kitchen, Louise whistled back—or tried to. Patsy, just waking up from her nap, held out her arms to be picked up. "Hi, Gal," he smiled as he lifted her out of her crib, warm from sleep.

Louise was rolling out pastry for a pie crust. "You're home early. Are you hungry? I was afraid you'd worked through lunch."

"No, the weather was so bad I just stopped in at the White Owl for a hamburger so I wouldn't have so far to walk back. Did the lights go out here? Some power lines were down in town and the lights are out."

"No," she answered. "We're okay, so far." She ran a knife blade around the edge of the pie pan, retrieving the surplus pastry that fell from it. "Want some coffee? I'm making a blackberry pie with some of the berries your mother put up last summer." She looked up at him and smiled.

He smiled and hugged her, Patsy caught between them. "I wonder if there's anything good on the radio."

The weather worsened during the night, with wind-driven sleet and freezing rain coating the city; ice-heavy tree branches fell, taking power lines down with them and soon almost all of Paducah was without electrical power. Candles and kerosene lamps were pressed into service.

H.B. made good use of the daylight coming in the window to work on some price cards for various shop-owners, but chaffed at the lost time in the sign shop.

The couple felt helpless and isolated, worrying about their families and unable to contact them. Louise became irritable and depressed and Patsy was fussy. When a utility truck rumbled down the street and stopped to make repairs along Adams Street they felt a surge of relief. But several days would pass before everyday living would resume.

CHAPTER

3

On the 4th day of January, 1937, life returned to something like normal.

That morning, H.B. dressed, brought in more coal for the stove and ate breakfast before going to work. A quart bottle of Dudley milk waited for them on the front porch. Thick cream had risen to the top and had frozen, forcing the little cardboard cap off at a rakish angle. He took the milk inside and put it in the little ice box in the kitchen. He checked the block of ice in its chamber and saw that it was melting a little, but not as fast as it would have done in warm weather. When the ice was almost gone they would put a cardboard sign in the front window indicating to the delivery man the size ice-block they would need.

Louise was busily collecting the dirty clothes to send to Paducah Laundry. Gathering up the clothes they had worn during the previous week along with towels and sheets, she bundled everything into a sheet and tied the corners together, pinning an itemized list to it. If the laundry truck driver could get there, he would pick up the laundry as he did every Monday and return it in a heavy brown paper bag the next day, "damp dried, with light starch in the shirts and dresses" at Louise's directions, ready to be ironed.

The wind had died down and the rain and sleet had stopped but the outside air was brittle with cold. He shrugged into his coat, kissed Louise and Patsy goodbye and set out for work. Ice or no ice, people were out and about that Monday morning. Power had been restored.

The Arcade Barber Shop was already open, a couple of patrons waiting their turn. Mrs. Treas was just putting her key in the door of her beauty shop and Joe Osheroff sat hunched over his sewing machine in his tailor shop near the lobby of the theatre.

There was some activity in the small area that would be occupied by the Pin Money Frock Shop. The walls were being freshly painted and boxes of merchandise stood on the floor as two women worked to get the shop ready to open in a few days.

The sign shop was just as he had left it. He picked up where he had left off, working intently to make up for lost time.

At the end of his workday he started home. The air seemed to have a little less bite in it and cinders had been scattered over the sidewalk to make for safer walking. The sky was dark but the street lights were back on and reflected drearily on the glazed pavement. It would be a long time until spring.

CHAPTER

4

The day dawned overcast and cold on January 5th. H.B. left for work and Louise had washed the breakfast dishes and cleaned the house. The light bill stood pigeon-holed in the secretary and she thought of errands delayed by last week's bad weather. Patsy had been cranky all morning. A little fresh air would do them both good, she thought.

She slipped out of her housedress and took an old blue wool dress from the wardrobe. Dressed, she combed her thick, dark hair, powdered her face and applied lipstick. Patsy was engrossed in some building blocks that had been a Christmas present from Pudgie and protested at having her play interrupted. She was consoled when Louise told her they were going downtown. She always enjoyed that.

Louise dressed her warmly, keeping her amused by singing to her. "Animal crackers in my soup..." she half sang, half hummed. She brought out the little red coat and leggings with zippers up the side of each leg. She coaxed her into the leggings, then picked her up and stood her on the dining table to put on her coat. Just as she buttoned the little coat up to her chin, Patsy, without warning, sat down on the table, sliding her leg under her.

Louise heard the sound before she saw the damage and her heart sank. She could hardly bear to look. There on the polished surface of her dining room table was a deep curved scratch from the zipper on Patsy's leggings. She stared at it in horror.

Putting Patsy back down, she raced to the kitchen for some

furniture polish. Surely she could polish it out. Surely it couldn't be that bad. But try as she might, the scratch remained. Tears welled up in her eyes and spilled over.

It's not even paid for yet, she protested to herself.

She no longer had the heart for the outing, but the light bill had to be paid and she needed to buy some darning cotton. She put on her coat, hat and gloves and maneuvered the stroller down the three steps to the sidewalk. Pushing the stroller along she punished herself, *Why did I stand her on the table? What was I thinking?* She had been so proud of that table and now it was ruined while it was still brand new. Maybe when they got home it would look better. Maybe it would seal back up. Maybe the polish hadn't had long enough to work. Maybe...

The fresh, cold air revived her spirits a little. She went directly to Kentucky Utilities Company and settled the light bill, then guided the stroller toward Kresge's Five and Ten Cent Store. Normally she would have enjoyed going up and down each aisle, seeing the array of goods to be bought for at most the tenth part of a dollar. Today, though, the merchandise remaining on the shelves and counters after Christmas looked tired and skimpy. The store was dismal, stripped of its Christmas decorations. The sales clerks were busy with inventory and there were few shoppers.

She found the darning cotton and paid the clerk five cents for two spools, one black, one brown. She remembered that H.B. had broken a shoestring that morning when he was getting dressed for work. He had managed to knot the broken ends but it might not hold much longer, frayed as it was in other places. She found another nickel in her purse and bought a new pair of shoelaces, receiving two cents back in change.

Moving on to the rear of the store, she lingered for a moment to leaf through a catalog of decal transfer designs. She was charmed by some colorful Dutch designs of windmills, tulips, little Dutch girls and boys in wooden shoes. In the spring, she would give their battered old wood kitchen table and chairs a fresh coat of white paint. She would try to save pennies and buy some of the decals to add color to the chair backs.

Nearby, a clerk lifted down a roll of oil cloth from several that hung on a rack against the wall and cut a length of it for a customer, the odor of linseed oil released as the shears separated the fabric with a faint hissing sound. She remembered that the oil cloth cover on the kitchen table was beginning to peel. New oil cloth in a cheerful pattern would add color to the kitchen and she made a promise to herself to buy some after she painted the furniture. Her spirits rose in anticipation of redecorating in the spring.

Finding another nickel in her purse, she waited her turn and then asked for a yard of unbleached domestic. Her old ironing board cover needed to be replaced and she would stretch the new fabric over it, tacking it in place underneath the wooden board.

Emerging from the bright lights of the store she saw that the clouds were darkening. She felt a twinge of disappointment. No trip downtown was ever complete for her without going to see the window displays at Rudy's Department Store. Better hurry home, though.

Turning the corner at 4th and Broadway, she almost collided with Henrietta Ellis, a friend and neighbor of her mother's from Madison Street. She wished that she could have avoided her. Mrs. Ellis was talkative and she was sure to bring up her mother's death. She didn't think she could face that. But Mrs. Ellis had been kind and helpful and had sat with them at the time of death. Now she swooped down on them and bent to coo at Patsy.

Linking her arm with Louise's, she said, "Ain't it cold today? I need a cup of coffee and you do, too." Louise was borne across the street and into Segenfelter's Drug Store, helpless to get away.

Mrs. Ellis steered them across the black and white tile floor, past the soda fountain to one of the little round marble-top tables with a monogram "S" in the center. Louise wondered if she had the price of a cup of coffee in her purse but Mrs. Ellis told her firmly to put her purse away. This was to be her treat.

Seated, Mrs. Ellis lifted Patsy from her stroller and settled her on her ample lap. "That's a mighty cheery red snowsuit you've got on, young lady." Louise was reminded of the damage that had been done by that snowsuit and found herself telling Mrs. Ellis about it.

Mrs. Ellis listened sympathetically and nodded, saying, "Well, that's a shame but things like that will happen. There's a-many these days that don't have a table to scratch."

With that, she dismissed the little tragedy and went on to regale Louise with news of her friends, Lily Mae and Jo Holland. Their late father had been master pilot of a river boat and Louise had pleasant childhood memories of going with Mrs. Holland and the girls to have Sunday dinner on the boat when it was docked at the foot of Broadway.

Louise sipped the hot coffee and found it comforting. She realized that her mind had wandered when she was brought back to the present by mention of her mother's name.

"Seems like it was about this time last winter when she passed, wasn't it? She was a pretty woman, was your mama, and your papa just doted on her. Mr. Harry don't look like he's feelin' too good these days. He's just not the same since your mama passed away."

She couldn't bear any more. She had to get away or she would start to cry right there in public. "Oh, Mrs. Ellis, thank you for the coffee. It was just what I needed but it looks like it might start raining any minute and I need to get Patsy home." The two women parted with warm promises to visit soon and Louise rushed home, arriving just ahead of the rain.

With the stroller safely on the porch, she opened the door and went in. She cast a sidelong glance at the dining table, hoping against hope that the scratch had somehow disappeared. It was, of course, still there. She felt heartsick.

Removing the offending snowsuit, she said, "Patsy, go play for a little while, and I'll fix us some lunch."

She opened the kitchen cabinet and took out a can of tomato soup. Taking a match from the holder on the wall above the stove, she struck it and held the flame to the burner. The gas jets came to life with a little puffing sound and she poured the soup in a saucepan to heat, stirring a blend of milk and water into it. There were still a few crackers in the box, but they would soon need more. *I'd better make a grocery list,* she thought.

After lunch, with Patsy settled down for a nap, Louise sat down with the basket of socks waiting to be darned. She threaded a darning needle with some of the brown cotton and slid her darning egg into a sock. Smoothing the hole over the darning egg, she sewed a running stitch around the edge of the hole, then worked the thread in long, straight stitches the width of the hole. Going back, she wove the cotton closely through the long stitches in a close basket weave. There. It would hold for awhile longer.

She sat listening to the rain as the pile of socks grew smaller. Some of them were her father's. Dorothy had a job as secretary in the office of Northwestern Mutual Life Insurance Company and said she didn't have time for darning. Louise thought she would take them out to his house the next nice day. She hadn't seen her father since Christmas and Mrs. Ellis's remark worried her.

Finished with the darning, she matched the socks together and rolled them in pairs. It was too early to think about starting supper. There was a piece of embroidery she had been working on at the bottom of the basket. She took it out and looked at it critically. Her grandmother, Ellen Stroud, had taught her to embroider and she had been an exacting teacher. Anything less than a perfect stitch had to be picked out with the point of a needle and done over. At the time, she had hated the lessons, but was glad now that she had learned. Living with Mammy Stroud in their home had not been without trials, but Louise had grieved for her when she died in 1924.

She removed the wooden embroidery hoops and placed them over a new section, stretching the linen firmly in place. This part of the pattern was to be worked in lazy-daisy stitches and French knots. When she finished the piece, she would crochet a border and use it as a dresser cloth. There was something soul-satisfying in the work and she enjoyed the sound of the rain.

She heard Patsy stirring in her crib. *Oh, Tish, don't wake up yet*, she thought. She sat very still and soon her child was quiet again. She worked quietly, enjoying the emerging pattern of colors. Finally, though, the small head bobbed up in the crib with a sleepy command, "Up!"

Louise put her work away and lifted Patsy from her crib. Together, they went to the kitchen and explored the cupboard. Not for the first time, Louise was grateful that her husband was easy to please. Tonight, there would be macaroni and cheese and stewed tomatoes for supper.

CHAPTER

5

The next morning the rain had stopped and, although the sun remained behind clouds, the air was noticeably warmer. Louise led Patsy across the front porch to the other side of the duplex and knocked on the door. There was no answer. She had meant to ask Mrs. Clark to let her use the telephone to order groceries but there was nobody at home.

Well, she thought, *we'll just go get them.* Patsy was mutinous when she again had to leave her blocks, but Louise promised her some little red cinnamon candies that could be bought for a penny a scoop.

Louise guided the stroller four blocks to Meacham's Grocery at the corner of 3rd and Kentucky Avenue. The grocery had a bell above the door that jangled energetically to announce the arrival of customers. Louise wondered why the bell was necessary. As always, Mr. Meacham stood behind the counter, thick arms folded over a canvas apron, a pencil behind his ear. He had a pleasant greeting for all who came in, kept a good variety of stock and would extend credit to the end of the month. The store was very clean and neat and, like almost all neighborhood groceries, smelled of a pleasant jumble of odors, impossible to identify singly. Louise would buy only what was needed for that day as she wouldn't be able to carry much and handle the stroller, too.

She gave Mr. Meacham her list and he quickly found the few items, going back to the meat case at the back of the store to measure a pound of hamburger meat, wrapping it in white butcher paper and tying it with string.

Mrs. Meacham came forward to write out the ticket, chatting pleasantly as she placed the groceries in a brown paper bag. Smiling at Patsy as she lifted the wooden lid of a large jar of cinnamon drops, she said, "I'll bet I know who these are for." She scooped out a penny's worth of the spicy sweets and poured them into a small white paper bag.

She gave Louise a carbon copy of the ticket, spearing the original on a spindle on the counter. She knew that H.B.would stop by on Friday evening to pay the bill. The bell jangled again as they left the store.

Taking a different route as a break in routine, Louise returned by way of South 3rd Street, guiding the stroller over the uneven brick sidewalk. Many of the sidewalks in Paducah were concrete now but a few of the old-fashioned brick sidewalks remained, as well as some cinder paths. The old bricks, laid in a herringbone pattern, were so worn that the edges were rounded off, a reminder of times past. Moss grew between the bricks and they could be slippery and treacherous so you had to watch your step. Patsy seemed to enjoy the jouncing ride.

A family who lived in an attractive bungalow near the corner of 3rd and Clark Street kept a parrot. She could hear it yelling raucously. "Listen, Patsy. That old parrot is saying 'Pretty Polly' — that silly thing," she laughed.

Maybe this would be a good day to walk out to Madison Street to see Dad. It was still early and she would take him his socks and they could have a nice visit. Patsy could have her nap out there while they visited.

Arriving home, Louise saw that the laundry had been delivered, the heavy brown paper bag leaning against the front door. She sighed. No visit today —the rest of her day would be spent at the ironing board. As she went in, she turned back to look at the suddenly darkening sky. More rain was on the way.

A look at the calendar that morning reminded H.B. that today was Mary Lee's birthday. At lunchtime he walked down to List's Drug Store to see her. She looked happy and well-placed behind the cosmetics counter, framed against the ornate oak interior.

H.B. was surprised to see Dick leaning against the counter in a leisurely posture. Mary Lee beamed at him. "Hi, Aitchy."

"Hi, yourself. Happy Birthday." Turning to Dick, he asked, "Aren't you supposed to be in school?"

"I've got a free period. I'm a senior, remember?" he replied defensively.

H.B. had had to drop out of school in his junior year for

Mary Lee Hargrove

three semesters. Their father had been laid off from his job and as the eldest it fell to him to get a job to help support the family. When he returned to school, his free periods had been spent in study hall, trying to catch up so that he could graduate in 1929.

"Mr. Jetton's gonna 'free period' you if he finds out you've been off the school grounds. You'd better get back while the gettin's good."

Dick scowled but straightened, said "So long, Sis. Happy Birthday," and

Dick Hargrove

sauntered toward the door, stopping, aggravatingly, to weigh himself on the big Toledo scales.

When he reached the door, H.B. called after him, "Say, Dick —come see us sometime."

Dick gave him an impudent grin, sketched a salute and replied, "Yeah, maybe I'll do that."

H.B. turned back to Mary Lee and shook his head. Dick was the youngest of the Hargrove brood and the only one of the four who resembled his mother's family, the Wrights. He was the apple of his mother's eye. H.B. thought that he needed a firm hand.

Mary Lee laughed. "Don't worry about Dick so much, Aitchy. He's kinda fresh but he'll be okay," she assured him.

"Are you having a nice birthday?"

"I sure am. I found out I'm being promoted to bookkeeper and I'm getting a nice raise."

"Aw, say, that's fine! That'll really help you out," he said, genuinely pleased for her.

"H. B.! How are you today?" Dr. Harry List had come to the front of the store to speak to him. "I saw Louise and Patsy at K.U. yesterday. Patsy stood up in her buggy and said 'Hi' to me, big as you please," he chortled.

Dr. Louis List called out a greeting from the Pharmacy. The two brothers were accorded the courtesy title of "Doctor" bestowed on many pharmacists in those days, and indeed were as knowledgeable as many doctors of their time.

"I'm glad you came in. I need to talk to you about some

price cards. I'll need some for the new merchandise coming in next week. Think you could handle that for me?"

It was a job that H.B. liked. The work could be tedious but he could do it at home in the evenings and Dr. List always paid a fair price. He lettered price cards for other businesses as well and the additional income helped.

He readily agreed and Dr. List asked, "Same price as last time?"

"Yes sir, same price." They shook hands again and Dr. List went back to his work.

H.B. turned back to say goodbye to his sister. "I hope you keep having a nice birthday, Mary."

"Thanks, I know I will. Mary Lena and Nell are taking me to Rothrock's for supper and we're going to see *After the Thin Man* at the Columbia afterward. This is Dish Night, too —maybe they'll draw my ticket number and I'll win a set of dishes for my hope chest."

"Maybe they will. Good luck. Well, I've got to go back to work. Tell the folks we'll be over to see them soon."

CHAPTER

6

Rain slashed the bedroom window for the fifteenth day in a row as Louise sat at the old treadle sewing machine that had been her mother's, a pile of mending in front of her. Patsy pulled at her mother's apron, pleading to go out. "No, Tish, we can't go out today. It's raining. Wait until I finish and we'll read a book."

Staying indoors for two weeks had been hard on both of them but she thought how much harder it was for H.B. to walk to and from work in this weather. She hoped his battered old black umbrella would hold up. Every evening she put his wet shoes under the coal stove to dry. The next morning they were curled and stiff, but dry enough to wear. He had been taking a lunch with him and she missed having that time with him at midday. The rain had continued almost without interruption since January 5th.

At last, she snipped the thread and put her sewing aside. Picking up a book of nursery rhymes, she took the little girl on her lap and made good on her promise.

H.B. left for work early that morning so he would have a

few minutes to walk down to the river. It had begun to rise noticeably after a sudden thaw on the 11th and now it was the 20th. The river reading yesterday was 46.2 feet, a rise of a foot and a half in twenty-four hours. In 1937, there was no floodwall or levee and an expanse of swollen river stretched out before him, east, north, south. The rain had abated somewhat to a thin, depressing drizzle. The atmosphere was warmish and murky and a kind of vapor hovered over the muddy water. Water stood in the street and along the gutters. Feeling uneasy, he stood for a few minutes watching a barge move sluggishly along. He was born in Graves County but had lived in Paducah since he was six years old and he had never seen the river look like this.

The rain picked up again as he turned to walk the five blocks back to the Arcade. A little over a mile to the west, gritty black smoke issued from the smokestacks at the Illinois Central Railroad Shops and the whistle sounded one long hoot, signaling the beginning of the workday. The heavy atmosphere kept the smoke almost parallel to the ground, guaranteeing a thick layer of soot for housewives to battle that morning.

Arriving at his shop, he immediately set to work on a lobby display, shutting out thoughts of the river and losing himself in his work.

CHAPTER
7

On Friday, January 22nd, H.B. had an appointment to have a tooth filled by his dentist, Dr. Lyman L. Duley. He sat down in the outer office to wait his turn. He could hear the shrill whine of the drill, then heard Dr. Duley instructing his patient to "spit, please."

Presently Nell, Dr. Duley's wife and office assistant, appeared at the green baize door and intoned "Next."

H.B. stood and strode manfully into the clinical little room, seating himself in the chair that was pumped up and down by a pedal at the base and was fitted with two padded disks that formed the headrest. Nell clipped a white napkin around his neck, topped it with a large drape and tilted the chair back, making H.B. feel completely at their mercy. Dr. Duley examined the tooth and administered a shot of Novocain, leaving H.B. to wait for the numbing effect.

As he sat waiting, he pondered the tray of instruments near the chair —hooks, picks, pincers, a little mirror. He supposed they had proper names, but he didn't particularly care what they were. As he eyed the drill hanging menacingly on his left, he heard people coming into the outer office. They were talking about the river.

A man with a loud voice announced, "There's a flood comin' and folks that live down yonder by the river are fixin' to get out." Another voice, an older one, by the sound of it, recalled the Flood of 1913 and wondered if they were in for it again. That was the flood that had set the standard by which all floods were judged in this community.

At length, Dr. Duley came back in. He, too, could talk of nothing else. Above the noise of the drill, he said, "Why, back in 1913 the water got almost up to the front steps of my Daddy's house. Let me tell you, it was a mess. Mr. Nagel showed me a picture of him and some other fellows standing out in the street at Third and Broadway and the water was up to their knees! Up to their knees!" he repeated for emphasis.

Unable to answer, H.B. grunted politely. Dr. Duley aimed a squirt of water at the newly excavated tooth. "Spit, please." H.B. leaned over the porcelain basin beside the chair and obligingly spat. Nell appeared at Dr. Duley's side with a little beaker of amalgam. It was always a relief when the procedure reached this stage. It was almost over. Dr. Duley pressed the filling into place. "Bite, but not too hard." Scraping at it a little, he instructed, "Now, bite again — not too hard."

Whipping the drape off, Nell unclipped the napkin and H.B. was set free. "Don't chew anything for a couple of hours," Dr. Duley admonished.

It was almost noon. No use thinking about lunch. He would have to wait until at least two o'clock. Well, he wasn't very hungry anyway. Maybe he would just wait until supper.

All that afternoon, everyone who came into the shop seemed preoccupied by the weather. He found it hard to concentrate on his work and had to discard a half-finished show card when he noticed a mistake.

"Dag-nab it," he muttered, tossing the ruined card into a waste basket. He turned his attention to a big lobby sign that had

Flood of 1913. William Nagel Sr. second from the left.

been brought in the night before. There would be plenty of time to paint it out before he went home. He hadn't used any stills on this one, so it would just be a matter of coating over the artwork.

Mr. Palmer appeared at the door. "H.B., I'm goin' home. It's rainin' pitchforks out there. Why don't you finish up here and I'll give you a lift." Accepting gratefully, H.B. put his paints away and stood the lobby sign upright. It would have to wait until to-morrow.

Louise had made a meatloaf, mashed potatoes and lima beans. H.B. suddenly felt hollowed out. He sat down at the table and bowed his head to say the blessing, holding his squirming daughter down in her highchair with one hand. "Dear Lord, we

Flood of 1913. 4th and Broadway.

thank Thee for these blessings. Pardon our sins, we ask for Christ's sake. Amen."

Filling his plate, he reached for a piece of light bread. The hot food tasted wonderful. He looked across the table at Louise and winked, noticing how pretty she looked in a blue housedress that matched her eyes. She winked back at him and smiled.

Patsy had stopped squirming and was dealing messily with a piece of bread and butter. She was learning to feed herself but still took milk in bottles.

As he finished his meal Louise brought out a freshly baked devil's food cake. It was a treat and he ate a big piece with another cup of coffee. The household budget didn't stretch to such desserts very often.

After supper he turned on the radio. There was a lot of static because of the weather. He turned the dial until at last he found a program they both liked. He went to the front door and looked out to see the rain coming down in sheets.

Louise was getting Patsy ready for bed when the radio program was interrupted. It was the first of what would be almost continuous weather bulletins.

He went in to kiss Patsy goodnight, seeing her settled in her crib with her Teddy bear. She fell asleep almost at once. Louise looked anxious. "Do you think we're really going to have a flood?"

"Well, some people seem to think so. I guess we should make some preparations in case we can't get out of the house for awhile."

They went to bed early but were unable to sleep. The rain pounded on the roof with increasing intensity. H.B. turned the bed lamp back on. Searching for distraction, he picked up a copy of *Anthony Adverse* that he had been reading aloud to Louise. He opened the book where it was marked and began reading. Louise propped herself up on her pillow to listen. He read several chapters, trying to ignore the sound of unrelenting rain.

Near midnight someone knocked at the front door. They looked at each other, startled. Going to investigate, H.B. saw that it was Otto Clark.

Anxiously, Otto asked, "Did you know the water's comin' up fast?" The two men talked for a minute; then H.B. came back to bed.

Louise was sitting up with the double wedding ring quilt pulled up to her chin, eyes wide with alarm. "Who was it?" she asked shakily.

"Otto Clark," he replied.

"What in the world did he want at this hour?"

H.B. turned out the light. "Well, Hon, he's worried about the water, too. Let's try to get some sleep. There'll probably be a lot to do tomorrow."

CHAPTER

8

The next morning the water was over the curb. There was no longer any doubt that there would be a flood. H.B. had been awake since daybreak, thinking about what he had heard of the 1913 flood, how people had managed and how best to prepare for it. The rain had stopped for the time being.

"Louise, if you'll make a grocery list, I'll go to the store. We'd better get enough food in to last a week."

She looked at him dubiously. "A week? You don't really think it'll last that long, do you?"

"I hope not. Do you remember hearing anybody say how long the flood lasted in 1913?"

"No, but I doubt that it was a whole week," she replied. "Still, I guess you're right. We'll use it all sooner or later anyway."

Louise was washing the breakfast dishes when she heard a knock at the door. Wiping her hands on a dish towel, she opened the door to her next-door neighbor. She smiled cordially and asked her in.

Mrs. Clark seemed hurried. "There's somebody on the telephone asking to talk to H.B. Will you tell him to come over?"

"He's not here right now. Do you suppose I could take the call?" Picking Patsy up, she threw a blanket around her and crossed the porch to the Clark's side.

"Hello?"

"Hello, this is Azalee Bolin at Rudolph's Grocery. Mrs. Hargrove asked me to call and tell H.B. that they're going to —"

The telephone crackled and went dead. Louise was left to wonder what she should tell H.B. They're going to do what? She wished she could have heard the rest of the message but there was no way to find out more. She thanked her neighbor and went back to her dishes.

Meacham's Grocery was closer to the river, so H.B. decided to go to Stubblefield's Grocery at the corner of 5th and Jackson Street, hoping to find shallower water in that direction. As soon as he reached the bottom porch step, his shoes were soaked.

The grocery was crowded with people and there was a pervasive feeling of anxiety. He bought carefully and when he left the store he had spent $7.00 —almost all the money he had —for two big bags of groceries.

On the walk home he picked his way cautiously, trying to organize his thoughts. He wished he had paid more attention when people talked about the last big flood. He felt sure there would be enough food but what else would they need?

Coal! The thought struck him with sudden force. He had noticed that morning that the heap was getting smaller and in a few days they would need to order more. He would have to bring in all that he could. Where would they put it?

Louise stood at the front door, watching for him. She took the bags of groceries from him. "Oh, Pill, look at you. Your shoes are soaked."

He tried to grin. "They were soaked as soon as I left the house. They're 'way past being soaked now."

"H.B., take your shoes right off and come in and get dry. You'll catch pneumonia."

"No use taking them off now. Meet me at the back door with the coal bucket. I want to get some more in while I can."

He sloshed around the side of the house, pushing aside the winter-withered Dorothy Perkins rose bush and a dead-looking lilac bush. The water was deeper back here.

Louise handed him the coal bucket, clucking at the condition of his shoes. He opened the door of the little coal shed and found the floor was slick with mud. Then he thought of kindling. The wood was wet. Well, he'd take it in and hope it would dry beside the coal stove. He noticed some stacks of bricks beside the shed. He had never known why they were there, but on an impulse he decided to move them to the front porch.

First he filled the coal bucket, emptied it on the little back porch and went back for another load, repeating the process until the back porch couldn't hold any more. One more bucket for the house for good measure and the coal was gone. The wind had changed, bringing sleet with it. He turned his attention to the bricks. His pant-legs were soaked to the knees and clung coldly to him. Making several trips, he transferred the bricks to the front porch.

Louise had rummaged in the bottom of the wardrobe and found an old pair of his shoes that were thought to be past wearing. They would have to do. She found pants, socks, and a towel and took them to him.

Stepping over the coal, he came in, shaky and famished from the exertion. He peeled off the wet garments, dried himself briskly and changed into the dry clothes.

"Go stand over there by the stove and get warm," Louise advised him. "I'll make us some lunch."

He watched her as she busied herself at the kitchen stove. Although she was usually a worrier, now she looked calm and efficient. She made sandwiches from warmed-over meatloaf, fried some potatoes and made a pot of coffee. She set the table and settled Patsy in her highchair. H.B. looked at the clock; it was only 11:30 but it seemed later. They ate almost in silence. Louise coaxed food into Patsy, at last giving up and letting her down to play.

H.B. ventured, "I hope the folks are okay."

Louise was reminded of the telephone call. "Oh, Pill, I forgot to tell you...Mrs. Bolin called the Clarks and asked for you. Since you weren't here, I went over and took the call. She said that your mother wanted her to tell you that they were going to do something but the connection was broken so I don't know what it was. I'm sure they're all right, though." She set a piece of last night's cake in front of him and refilled his coffee cup. The food restored him. "You know, this may not be so bad after all," she said cheerfully. "We can just stay at home and read and listen to the radio. We'll be 'as snug as three bugs in a rug'."

They had both avoided looking outside, fearing what they might see, but now could no longer resist going to the window. They were shocked to see how the water had advanced on the house. The radio broadcast almost unbroken bulletins on flood conditions. Louise picked Patsy up and put her in her crib for a nap. She lay wide-eyed, clutching her Teddy bear.

H.B. was still standing at the window. He had not told her that Otto Clark had said last night that the river was predicted to reach fifty-four feet. He turned to her, looking worried. "Hon, I don't mean to worry you but I think maybe we should try to do something with the furniture."

"Why, what do you mean?" she asked.

"Well, the water's coming up pretty fast. If it should get in the house —I don't think it will, but if it should —we'd have some damage."

Louise's composure vanished. "What can we do?" she asked, her voice rising in alarm.

They were a young married couple, both just twenty-seven years old. They had not been able to accumulate much of value. Besides their bed, dresser and wardrobe, there was the secretary, the dining room suite, a cedar chest, a second-hand radio, a banjo clock. A make-shift bookcase held their treasured books. And, there was the old sewing machine. Patsy's crib, a tired-looking sofa, a chair or two and the kitchen table and chairs had all been bought second-hand.

H.B. thought of the bricks. Bringing them in, they stacked them three-high and set the dining table on top of them, the chairs on top of the table. Louise ran her hand over the scar on the table. That day seemed like a long time ago. They took the books from the bookcase and stacked them on the mantle. The tall secretary defied rescue. Louise remembered a new salmon pink dress she had made last summer, along with the rest of their summer clothes that were stored in the cedar chest. More bricks raised the cedar chest and the sewing machine. The remaining furniture was raised or stacked together.

They had done all they could. They paced the floor, anxious and bewildered. Someone knocked at the door. It was Otto Clark again.

"Say, H.B., we're gettin' out. Don't you all have some place to go? We'll be glad to take you somewhere, but if you don't get out now you're gonna be trapped."

They looked at each other in stunned disbelief. Could this really be happening? Fighting panic, they decided quickly to go to Louise's father's house, comparatively far from the river.

H.B. threw a few necessities into a small suitcase as Louise dressed Patsy warmly in her snow suit and folded a blanket around her. Hurrying back to the kitchen, she filled a baby bottle with milk. She snatched up the Teddy bear and gave it to Patsy. They put on their coats and hats, then stepped out on the porch, closing the door behind them.

Otto and Mrs. Clark and their nine-year old daughter, Barbara, waited for them as the car idled in the street. They had secured some suitcases to the top of the car with rope. Otto got out of the car to help Louise down the flooded steps and down the walk. H.B. followed, carrying Patsy. Otto took the suitcase and settled it among the others. They crowded into the old car. Barbara fretted about her friends, Charlene Hill and Barbara Brown, who lived in the same block. She held out her arms, asking if she could hold Patsy.

After an attempt at polite conversation they drove mostly in silence, praying that the motor wouldn't stall. Otto threaded his way through the flooded streets, instinctively turning away from areas where he judged the water to be too deep. Some city workers wearing hip-waders were beginning to place signs at intersections where the streets were impassable. The land nearest the river was

relatively flat and the water level was consistent. As they drove west it was harder to tell. In a few areas the elevation was high enough that the ground was still visible; in others the water was dangerously deep.

At 17th and Broadway, Otto started to turn the car north on Fountain Avenue. H.B said, "Wait a minute, Otto. Stop here. We can get out and walk the rest of the way. It's not very far and you need to get your family to a safe place."

"Aw, H.B., stay put. We can take you all on over there."

But H.B. and Louise, holding Patsy, were already getting out of the car. H.B. retrieved the suitcase from the top of the car. Her voice quivering, Louise said, "I don't know how we can ever thank you. What would we have done without you all?"

Mrs. Clark reached out to hug her. The two women had been cordial, but not close; at this time of parting, not knowing when they would see each other again, their neighbors seemed very dear. Mrs. Clark patted Patsy's hand. Otto reached across the car seat to shake hands with H.B. There was nothing more to say. They watched as the old car traveled west on Broadway, soon disappearing in the mist.

CHAPTER

9

During their courtship and since their marriage, they had walked on Fountain Avenue countless times, enjoying the beauty of the surroundings, the stately homes under arching trees. Lang Park was a familiar haunt to them. As a child, Louise had played there with her friends, Lily Mae and Jo, circling the park on roller skates until darkness drove them home. After they met in high school, H.B. often walked out to Louise's house on Sunday afternoons and they had strolled in the park, meeting friends, taking snapshots with an old Kodak box camera, sharing good times, falling in love.

But today was different. The houses looked closed off and unfriendly. The bare tree branches snatched at the low clouds and the statue of General Tilghman was barely visible in the mist. The sleet grew heavier and it was slippery underfoot. Water was standing in the street and inching its way up into the yards. It was late afternoon now and beginning to get dark. Reaching Madison Street, they saw that it looked impassable.

"Let's try the alley. Maybe that'll be a little better."

H.B. had been carrying Patsy, who had fallen asleep with her head on his shoulder, but now he handed her off to Louise and walked a little ahead of them, feeling his way along for a safe path. Their feet felt like blocks of ice in their sodden shoes. Finally they reached their destination, too tired even to think. They crossed the yard and entered the house through the back door.

H.B. and Louise courting in Lang Park, 1929.

Dorothy bustled around to find dry clothes for them. In their haste they had forgotten to pack night clothes. Harry found an old flannel bath-robe for H.B. and Louise changed into one of Dorothy's nightgowns and a smock. Their clothes were spread to dry in front of the fireplace in the living room. Patsy was fed, bathed and put down to sleep in Dorothy's bed.

Together, Louise and Dorothy prepared a meal. At the supper table, Dorothy spilled over with questions that they were too exhausted to answer. Harry sat quietly, eating little, lost in thought.

After supper, Dorothy made up the bed in the spare room. The room had been closed off to save the cost of heating it and it felt damp and chilly. She put a hot-water bottle in between the sheets. H.B. and Louise sank gratefully into bed, huddled under the quilt and waited for sleep. But, tired as they were, sleep eluded them. Their minds churned with anxiety over what the next day might bring.

"H.B.?"

"What, Hon?"

"Do you suppose the water's gotten into our house?"

"I don't know. Maybe it won't be too bad."

"It'll ruin the floor if it does. When do you think we'll get to go home?"

"It'll probably be a few days. I wish I knew how to get in touch with the folks to let them know we're okay."

H.B. sat up in bed suddenly. "Oh, gosh. I should have paid the bill at Meacham's yesterday."

Louise sighed, "Well, Hon, you can't do anything about it now. They know we'll pay as soon as we can. They might not have been there anyway, with the water being so high."

They grew quiet and finally slept a little.

Louise awoke to hear the mantel clock strike one o'clock. H.B. had gotten up and was looking out the window. The water had risen noticeably since they went to bed and the back yard was inundated. They wouldn't have been able to reach the house by that route now.

Louise slipped into Dorothy's smock and crossed the hall. She could hear her father snoring heavily in the next room. She tiptoed into Dorothy's bedroom to check on Patsy. She was fast asleep, her arm flung across her Teddy bear. Dorothy lay awake beside her. She touched her fingertip to her lips and got out of bed quietly. Putting on a chenille robe, she led the way to the kitchen. She touched the light switch on the kitchen wall. There was no electrical power. Louise found a kerosene lamp in the pantry, lit it and put it on the kitchen table.

Dorothy tried to light a burner on the gas stove, but there was no response there, either.

"Well, I was going to make us a cup of tea but I guess that's out. Goodness only knows what we'll do about breakfast. We might as well go back to bed and try to get some sleep."

They slept only fitfully until daybreak. H.B. was up and dressed at first light. Looking out the window, he saw that the water had continued to rise and the houses across the street were reflected on the surface. It was unnaturally quiet. He went to check the supply of coal in the bin on the back porch, filled a bucket and took it to the living room. The fire in the fireplace had gone out and the room was icy. He stoked the coal stove that served to warm the rest of the house, shook down the ashes and filled the coal chamber, poking the embers to life. He went back to the fireplace and, without taking time to sweep out the ashes, put some coal in the grate. Time enough for house-keeping when the chill was off.

"You're up early." Dorothy appeared at the door. "Don't light the fire until I've swept those ashes out."

He sat back on his heels. Dorothy could be bossy, but this was no time to have words with her. He reached for the hearth broom and shovel.

"I'll take care of it. I just wanted to get the house warmed up before everybody else gets up."

Louise was in the kitchen searching for something to make for breakfast. With no electricity and no gas, it would be a skimpy meal. Dorothy put a pot of coffee on top of the coal stove, hoping it would brew, and set some eggs in a saucepan full of water beside it. There was bread, butter, and a little fruit. Dorothy produced a couple of old toasting forks from the pantry and Louise went into the living room to toast some bread at the fireplace.

At the breakfast table they studiously avoided talking about the water. Patsy, happy to be with her grandfather and her Aunt Dot, ate some buttered toast and part of a banana without protest.

Louise noticed that her father's hand shook when he held his coffee cup and he seemed to shuffle a little when he walked. Why, she wondered, hadn't she noticed these things before?

"Dad, are you feeling all right?"

"I'm all right, honey. Don't worry about me. But I didn't sleep a wink last night."

Dorothy retorted, "Well, it certainly sounded to me like you were sleeping. You were snoring like a grampus."

Louise glanced at her reproachfully. H.B. cleared his throat. "You know, we spent yesterday afternoon putting our furniture out of harm's way. We'd better get to work and do the same thing out here."

Harry put down his napkin and pushed his chair back. "That sounds like a good idea. I'll help you."

Louise was wiping Patsy's face and hands with a damp cloth. "Wait a minute, Dad. I think it would help more if you would take care of Patsy and keep her out of the way." She felt that her father was too feeble to move furniture and nothing would please Patsy more than to have her grandfather's undivided attention.

As Dorothy cleared the table, she turned and said, "I don't think we need to worry about the furniture too much. The water surely isn't going to get deep enough 'way out here to get into the house."

Harry went into the living room and sat down in his wicker rocking chair in front of the fireplace. Louise led Patsy in and he lifted her to his lap. A storybook and her Teddy bear would keep her occupied for awhile.

"All right Patsy," Harry said. "What shall we read? Here's *Red Raspberry Jam*. How would that be?"

Harry Dalton

Dorothy Dalton

CHAPTER 10

"Mama, come quick! Look who's coming!" Mary Warren danced with excitement as she looked out the window of Ondine and Frank's house, a large gray cat in her arms.

Nannette and Ondine both went over to the window. A rowboat bearing the rest of the family made its way down Harrison Street and pulled around to the front porch of 501 Fountain Avenue.

"Frank! Ralph!" Ondine called. "You all come help."

The boatman tethered the rocking, barely adequate boat to the porch rail and Frank and Ralph emerged from the kitchen. H.B. lifted his wailing child out and handed her to Mary Warren.

Ondine laid an old rag rug on the icy porch as Frank and Ralph helped the others safely out of the boat. "Wipe your feet good," she admonished. "I don't want any mud on my clean floor."

With some asperity Frank said, "Ondine, will you quit worrying about the floor?"

"Come on in and get warm. No telling how long we'll be able to stay here, though. It looks like the ol' river's gonna get our house, too, sooner or later," Frank said.

"No, now Frank," Ondine protested. "The water's not gonna get that high."

The little house was warm and cozy, but only comfortable for a small family. Now it would be pressed to accommodate eight

Frank and Ondine Dalton

adults and two children. Frank helped Harry, stiff with cold, to a chair by the fire where a kettle of soup simmered on a makeshift grill, filling the room with the good odor of meat stock and vegetables.

Mary Warren chattered excitedly, "The lights are out and so is the gas and Mama and Ondine are cooking soup in the fireplace, just like pioneers!"

"How long have you all been here?" Dorothy asked Ralph. "We saw your car at the curb and it doesn't look like you'll be going anywhere in it any time soon."

"We came over to pick Mar' War'n up last night, and before we knew it the water was in the car. We spent yesterday afternoon takin' our customers' clothes out of the plant and storin' 'em upstairs at our house. I'm just gettin' started in my own business and I can't afford to have people sayin' I didn't take care of their clothes. We slept in chairs over here last night."

"Well," Ondine said, "we ought to have enough food for a day or two. Frank and Ralph put on hip waders and went down to the corner grocery store this morning. Seems like everybody else had the same notion and the store was so full of people they couldn't get waited on. They finally had to just pick up what they could and left some money beside the cash-register. I'll make some more soup and we can have some cheese sandwiches. I don't reckon we'll starve before the water goes on back down."

"Where shall I put this suitcase?" Dorothy inquired.

Louise looked around. "Oh, that's right. Pill, where's our suitcase?" H.B. looked stricken.

"Hon...I must have left it on the front porch at your Dad's house. I meant to pick it up but in all the confusion I guess I just forgot it."

For a moment Louise was dumbfounded. They stared at each other, aware that at that moment they might own nothing in the world but the clothes they were wearing. She turned away and began to cry.

"Well, you're not by yourselves," Nannette laughed. "We

61

spent all that time taking care of our customers' clothes, and now we don't have anything of our own, either."

"Now, Honey," Ondine admonished Louise, "stop cryin' and come on in the kitchen and help me cut up some more vegetables. No use grievin' over what you can't help."

"Why is Louise crying?" Mary Warren whispered to her mother. "She'll be all right," her mother replied. "Go on and play. Want a cracker? Take one for Patsy, too."

H.B. went out to the front porch. After the hot, crowded house, the cold air felt refreshing. All that morning they had watched boats carrying evacuees passing the house on Madison Street. Early in the afternoon they had realized that they would have to leave, too. He had stepped out on the icy front porch and hailed a passing boat and they had become refugees.

He watched the water lapping against the clapboard of the house next door. It was noticeably deeper than it had been when they had first arrived just a little while ago. Looking south toward Lang Park, he saw a Goldbloom Milk wagon that had been abandoned, the horse unharnessed and taken to safety. Somewhere in the distance a cow bawled for its calf and a church bell rang dolefully. The tree branches were glazed with ice and there was a heavy atmosphere of desertion.

Louise came out on the porch and linked her arm in his.

He asked, "Mad at me?"

"Not much," she replied. "I don't know what we're going to do, though. I guess there really wasn't enough in that little old suitcase to help out for long anyway, was there?"

The door opened and Ralph joined them. "There's not enough room in that house to swing a dead cat," he said. They stood watching as snow and ice floated on the muddy water lapping at the top step. Ondine stuck her head out the door.

"Does it look like it's started to go down any?"

"Not so's you'd notice, Ondine," Ralph replied.

"Well, you all come on in and have some soup before you freeze to death. I don't think it's coming up as fast as it was...do you?" she asked dubiously.

"Look over there. What do they want?" Two or three people stood at an upstairs window of a house diagonally across the street.

Through cupped hands a young man shouted, "Come on over here with us." Frank shouted back, "Can't do it. No way to get over there."

"That's the Mitchells," he explained. "I reckon they plan on waitin' it out upstairs. Wish we could get over there."

Frank looked up from his soup. "Hush, you all...be quiet for a minute." He cocked his head in the direction of the front door. "Never mind. I thought I heard somebody —wait, there it is again."

The group listened intently. "I don't hear anything, Frank," Ondine said.

Then they heard a distant call. "Hey!!!"

The whole family hurried to the front door.

Again, the call, "Hey!!!"

The water had reached the edge of the porch. A little man in hip waders stood below it holding a rope attached to a tiny row-boat. Bundled into a thick plaid coat, he wore an old hunting cap, the earlaps standing out at a 45 degree angle from his ears, and his nose was crimson from cold.

"Y'all come on and I'll carry you over yonder acrost the street in my boat."

Ralph stifled a laugh.

Frank, mindful of the little man's good intentions, said, "Friend, that's a mighty small boat. We sure do appreciate your offer but I think we'll wait around awhile longer." Ondine peered over Frank's shoulder.

"Now, Frank, that water's gettin' awful high. I think we

oughta go with him." Dorothy muttered, "Nothing doing," and herded Mary Warren and Patsy back into the warmth of the house, with Louise and Nannette following. A strong gust of wind tossed the little boat and icy water slapped against Ondine's feet. "Well," she said, her voice rising in panic, "I'm goin'."

Resolutely, Ondine, tall, big-boned and stout, gathered her old tweed coat around her and stepped deliberately toward the little craft. She did not notice what had just become apparent to the three men standing on the porch with her.

"Wait a minute, Ondine!" —"Look out, there's water!" — "Don't get in that boat!" The warnings, given in a garbled unison, were lost on her as she stepped into the leaking boat. It immediately sank under her weight as she whooped frantically, the water rising around her knees. She burst into tears of outrage and humiliation.

The little man regarded her with a grieved expression. "Ma'am…you sunk my boat," he reproached her.

"I didn't either sink your fool boat," Ondine bawled. "It was about to sink anyway and you let me get right in it!"

Frank and H.B. helped her back up to the porch and she retreated into the house, trailing flood water across the floor.

Crestfallen, the little boatman mumbled, "I'll have to go get me another boat." Abandoning the boat, he trailed off through the water and disappeared into the mist.

CHAPTER

11

Water was observed seeping under the baseboard onto the bathroom floor. They had spent the afternoon watching the water rising against the clapboard of the house next door. Several boats filled with evacuees had passed by and now it was beginning to get dark. Any hope they had of staying in the house vanished. Dressing warmly, and hastily gathering up what they thought they could take with them, they went out to the front porch. Mary Warren held the gray cat in her arms.

"Mother, what's gonna happen to Tom?" she asked tremulously.

"Now, Honey, we can't take the cat with us. There won't be room and he wouldn't like it in the boat anyway."

"You mean he has to stay here in the water? He'll drown." Tears threatened to overflow.

Ralph answered, more sharply than he had intended, "Mar' War'n, put that animal back in the house. You heard your mother."

Frank muttered, "Where the heck have all the boats gone? I haven't seen one since we came out on the porch."

Ondine craned over the porch rail and stared in the direction of Lang Park. "I don't see any...wait, yes, I do. Bo-o-at! Bo-o-at! Come get us, boat!" A johnboat appeared in the distance, moving slowly against the current.

Mary Warren disappeared back into the house and emerged again holding the cat in her arms. Close to tears, she said, "Daddy, we just can't let poor old Tom stay here and get drowned, can we?"

Nannette said, "Honey, they don't ever let people take pets with them when something like this happens."

"Why not?" the child asked, gulping back tears.

"Well, they have to have room for all the people who need to go in the boats and they don't have enough room for pets." She hesitated, then said, "Go get me that old blanket from the chair." She bundled the struggling cat into the blanket and said, "I don't think this will work, but we'll do the best we can. Hold still, Tom." Surprisingly, the cat settled down in the warm folds of wool and went to sleep.

Impatient with the boat's slow progress, Ondine again leaned out into the twilight and shouted, "Bo-o-at, hurry up and come get us, boat!"

A familiar voice called back, "What's the matter, Ondine? 'Fraid you're gonna get your feet wet?"

Almost overcome with relief, Ondine once more burst into tears. "Oh, it's my brother comin' to get us. Hurry up, Eugene, we're waitin'."

After what seemed an eternity, the boat pulled up to the front porch. Eugene was not alone. Their brother, Pete, sat in the boat, occupied with lighting a couple of lanterns. The last of the daylight had by now disappeared and the feeble light from the lanterns only made the darkness more oppressive.

Eugene tethered the boat to the porch rail with a rope. "How many've you got?" he inquired. "Looks like we're gonna need more than one boat. Maybe another'un is close enough to hear me whistle." He put his fingers to his lips and whistled piercingly. Recognizing the rest of the family, he said, "Hidy, folks. Seems like a long time since I saw you all."

Eugene and Pete Mabry worked with the Civilian Conservation Corps, a public relief program under President Franklin D. Roosevelt's New Deal administration. Its purpose was to provide employment for men who were out of work because of the Depression. The program maintained a large camp on the north side of

Paducah in an area bounded by North 23rd and North 27th Streets and by Clay and Harrison Streets. In normal conditions, the men employed by the CCC were kept busy with building, digging ditches, or any useful task that came to hand.

They lived in barracks they had built for themselves. Most men were paid about $30.00 a month, with all but $5.00 of it being sent home to their families, leaving them with that small allowance for personal needs. Now, they were fully occupied with building and manning boats to ferry the flood victims to safety.

"No use waitin' around. We need to start loadin' you all on. Somebody else'll get here directly. Mr. Dalton, let's get you in the boat."

Straightening his shoulders, Harry said, "No, thanks. You know the rule. Women and children first."

Dorothy spoke up. "Wait a minute. We need to stay together. Why don't we wait for another boat?"

"Oh, let's not wait any longer. We have to get the children to safety. We'll all wind up at the same place anyway. By the way, where are we going?" Louise asked.

Eugene replied, "Everybody's goin' out to 28th and Broadway. That's where the high water stops, so far. There's only one road open out of Paducah, and that's Highway 45."

"Out of Paducah...do you mean we have to leave town?"

"Well, unless you know somebody you can stay with out yonder. I heard they've let out the schools, and they're gonna let people stay in 'em 'til the water goes down."

This introduced a new problem. Somehow, they hadn't given a thought to what they would do beyond escaping from the rising flood water.

Ondine announced, "Well, I want to go to Cunningham. If we can find a way to get there, everybody can go out there with us."

Cunningham was a village in Carlisle County, about thirty-five miles from Paducah. It had been Ondine's home until she and Frank were married. Her father, step-mother and two little half-sisters lived there still.

At that moment another boat rounded the corner. "Hey, Eugene, you need some help?" called a voice out of the darkness.

"Hey, Joe Ed. Who've you got with you?" Eugene asked.

"This here's Bubba. He's gonna help us out…I hope." The last two words were uttered under his breath. He held up his lantern and set it on the porch. "Okay, who's goin' first?"

It soon became apparent that there would be no room in either boat for suitcases or any other belongings. Dorothy opened her suitcase quickly and retrieved a little bag of jewelry that had belonged to their mother, pinning it to the inside of her coat pocket. She closed the suitcase and pushed it to the back of the front porch, then was helped into a waiting boat.

Away from the meager shelter of the front porch, they felt the bitter cold more keenly than ever. The snow had stopped but the water was crusted with ice. A brief break in the cloud cover allowed enough moonlight to show that the tree branches were thickly encased in ice and a dusting of sleet and snow lay over all. The boats, heavy with passengers, rode low in the water. As the men pulled away from the house, they were again rowing against a swift current. They headed first to 21st and Harrison Street, a matter of about four blocks.

As the boat manned by Joe Ed and Bubba rounded the corner to go south on 21st Street, it swung sharply, struck a utility pole and tilted, icy water splashing over the side. Dorothy and Louise screamed, Patsy began to cry and Joe Ed swore pungently.

"*Boy, ain't you ever handled a boat before?*" he bellowed at Bubba.

Harry spoke sharply, "Joe Ed, watch your language. There

are ladies present." Louise, speechless with shock, covered Patsy's ears with her gloved hands.

"S'cuse me, ladies," Joe Ed mumbled in apology.

"Everybody okay over there?" Eugene called across the water. The other boat had drawn close enough that they could dimly see the anxious faces of Ondine, Frank, Ralph, Nannette and Mary Warren, snuggled between her mother and her aunt, pale and frightened in the lantern light.

"We got it under control," Joe Ed responded.

H.B. put his arm around Louise as she leaned against him, crying quietly. Nobody spoke. There was no sound except for the scrape of the oars in their holders and the splash of the water.

Dorothy finally broke the silence. "I wonder what time it is."

Harry replied, "Even if I could get my watch out, I wouldn't be able to see it. It must be getting late, though."

They fell quiet again, too tired and bewildered to think clearly. The boat continued its slow, clumsy progress down North 21st Street. Occasionally the clouds thinned enough that the full moon illuminated the darkened houses along the street. The lanterns on the boats were reflected briefly in the windows.

As they at last neared Jefferson Street, they heard the welcome sound of human activity. They heard the noise of a heavy motor and the sound of voices before they were able to see a large scow at the corner of 21st and Jefferson. Eugene's boat was already there and his passengers were being helped aboard the scow.

Joe Ed turned to them. "Here's where ya'll get off, folks. This is as far as I can take ya. You get on this ol' scow and th' tractor'll pull y'all on out to where you're goin'. Good luck," was Joe Ed's farewell address. He helped Dorothy out of the rocking boat as H.B. took Patsy from Louise.

When they were all on board the scow Dorothy looked around, accounting for the family. "Where's Ralph?" she demanded.

Nannette replied, "Our boat was so crowded that Pete stayed behind. Eugene's going back to get him and Ralph said he'd

Mary Warren "Pudge"

go with him."

Louise asked anxiously, "How will he know where to find us?" A glance at Mary Warren made her regret her question. The child looked worried.

"Pudgie, come sit over here by me," Dorothy invited. "Don't you worry about your Daddy. He's just like an ol' hound dog. He can find anything." Mary Warren willingly moved over beside her Aunt Dot, nestling against her for warmth.

Louise patted her knee. "How about holding Patsy for a few minutes. My arms are about to go to sleep." Patsy, awake now and ready to play, was content to sit on her cousin's lap. A game of patty-cake kept her entertained until Louise produced the baby bottle she had filled with milk for her in Ondine's kitchen.

Nannette whispered to Louise, "I'm surprised nobody's asked what's in this blanket. This cat's so quiet I just hope it hasn't suffocated in there."

She cautiously lifted one corner of the blanket and was rewarded by Tom's opening one amber eye and meowing. She quickly covered the cat again and tried to appear nonchalant.

Louise laughed. "That cat sure will have a story to tell his grandchildren, won't he?" she whispered.

"When's this thing gonna start movin'?" Ondine asked. "I'm so tired I can't see straight."

Ralph and Nannette Dalton

Frank tried to shift his position in the crowded craft. "Matter of fact, I think we are moving. It's just so slow you can't tell it. Lord, it's cold. Dad, don't go to sleep," he admonished Harry.

"I won't, but I tell you I'd give anything I own just to lie down in my own bed right now," Harry answered.

"What I want is a hot bath and a change of clothes," Dorothy announced. Then she recalled that all of their clothes had been left behind. She sighed deeply. "I just can't imagine what we're going to do."

Nannette regarded her for a moment and replied, "Well, we're all in the same predicament. I'm glad Mary Warren's wearing that little dress with the pinafore. I can wash her dress and she can wear the pinafore with her sweater over it, and then the other way around. It won't be so easy for the rest of us though."

Mary Warren leaned her head on her mother's shoulder sleepily. "I hope my new bike will be okay," she murmured.

All at once they were all startled by a heavy scraping sound at the side of the scow.

"What on earth was that?" Dorothy almost shrieked.

Frank replied, "I think the scow just scraped over a car underwater. See that pole sticking up over there? Eugene said they're poking those through the tops of cars that've been left on the street

71

so people in motor boats will see 'em and steer clear."

"Why, that will just ruin the tops of those cars, won't it?" Dorothy asked indignantly.

H.B. and Frank laughed. Frank said, "Yeah, that's a real shame, all right," then began to laugh again.

"What's so funny?" Ondine demanded.

Suddenly, they all began to laugh uproariously without knowing why. Then, as suddenly, they grew quiet.

CHAPTER 12

Time passed slowly and the night deepened. At last they saw the railroad overpass in the distance. Some trucks were parked on dry land nearby. The scow drew up to a wooden platform and a man appeared, holding out his hand to help the family out of the scow.

They were stiff with fatigue, and unsteady on their feet. Seeing Nannette, the man gallantly offered, "Ma'am, let me take your baby." Too tired and too surprised to resist, she let the man take charge of the bundled blanket.

Tom, sensing the change of ownership, stuck his head out of the blanket, yowling loudly in protest as he struggled to escape. The man almost dropped the bundle in his shock. "Oh, my gawd, it's a cat!" He sneezed twice and hastily handed Nannette's "baby" back to her.

He turned to Dorothy and offered his hand, then lifted Pudgie out. When Louise stepped up to mount the platform, she stumbled and the almost empty baby bottle fell from her hand, struck the edge of the scow, then dropped into the muddy water with a final sounding "plunk" and floated away. "Oh, no," she protested. "Oh, no."

"Well, Hon," H.B said, "We've been talking about when we ought to wean her from that bottle, so I reckon now's the time."

H.B. and Frank helped Harry out of the scow, with Ondine supporting him from behind. "Ya'll just go on over to them trucks.

73

Evacuation Point, 28th and Boradway.

They'll carry you over to the drug store. That's where folks go to warm up and wait for somebody to come get 'em," the man instructed as he turned away to another task.

The trucks were not far away, but tired as they were it might as well have been a mile. They trudged the short distance, glad to be on dry land again. Another man was on hand to help them into a truck.

Three or four other people were already on board, engaged in earnest conversation. They glanced up and acknowledged them with a nod, but went on talking. "Like I was a-sayin', I'm worried about Aunt Ider. She says she seen a cow on somebody's upstairs porch," an anxious-looking middle-aged woman said to the man beside her. The man looked at her in astonishment, then turned to an elderly woman on his other side.

"Now, Aunt Ider, you know you never seen—"

"I know what I seen, and I seen a cow on a upstairs porch," Aunt Ider shrilled indignantly. "I seen it as plain as I see you!"

Turning back to the first woman, he said, "We're all plumb

Refugee Runway, near Keiler Park.

tuckered out. A body could think they seen just about anythin'. When we get where we're goin', see if you can git her to lay down awhile."

The door of the truck cab slammed shut and the motor coughed into action. It was an uncomfortable but mercifully short ride to Albritton's Drug Store. The drug store offered the amenity of a pot-belly stove and the family crowded around its welcome warmth. Blinking in the unaccustomed light, Frank blew on his hands and rubbed them together. "Well," he wondered aloud, "What next?"

"I thought there'd be more people in here," Dorothy observed.

A woman standing behind the counter said, "If you'd'a been here a couple of hours ago, you'd'a seen a right smart of 'em. Most of 'em went on over to Clark School, but I reckon the school's about full up. There's some CCC fellas that'll carry you somewhere when they get back with their cars. There might still be some room at Arcadia School. The Red Cross folks've been out here too, givin' typhoid shots, but they're gone 'til mornin'. We thought we were about done for the night 'til you all came in."

Harry pulled out his pocket watch. "Almost twelve-thirty. I thought it was later, though. I guess you must be pretty tired, too. We'll get out of your way as soon as we can," he assured her kindly.

"Oh, somebody'll prob'ly be here all night, in case some more come in," she replied.

Ondine had been peering out the window. "Here comes a car now," she exclaimed. An old car pulled up outside the drugstore, followed by another. Frank and H.B. went outside to speak to the drivers.

Ondine, on tenterhooks, followed them to the door. "Frank, ask 'em if they're CCC. If they are, mention Eugene and Pete," she instructed, hoping the connection might give them an advantage.

In a few minutes, H.B. came back in. "They've offered to give us a lift. Frank says we can all go down to Cunningham and make our plans from there." Ondine was elated and immediately started herding the family toward the cars.

H.B. lingered behind to speak to Louise. "Hon, I don't know what else we can do, but I don't see how the Mabrys are going to have room for all of us. What do you think?"

Before Louise could answer, Ondine grabbed their arms and pulled them toward the door. "You all come on right now and maybe we'll be on time for breakfast."

CHAPTER
13

There followed a long, roundabout ride over dark and ice-rutted country roads to the Mabry home in Cunningham. Modern utilities had not yet found their way to the little village in early 1937. Indoor plumbing was an undreamed-of luxury and oil and kerosene lamps provided the only light after nightfall.

Cunningham was still asleep when the family arrived, but there was lamplight at the Mabry house. Ondine's father, Nick, carried a rural postal route and literally got up with the chickens. Burdette was in the kitchen, getting ready to cook an enormous breakfast of pork chops with cream gravy, fried potatoes, eggs, grits, biscuits and coffee. Nick stood at the door, his frame filling the lighted doorway.

"Come on in, folks," he greeted them as genially as if it had been four in the afternoon rather than four in the morning. "Come on in and make yourselves to home."

Nannette, more than ready to be relieved of Tom, let him jump down from her arms. Tom bounded off into the darkness and disappeared.

Burdette, wiping her hands on her apron, came smiling into the front room. "We're real glad you all came. I hope you're hungry. Breakfast will be ready in a little while. Just take off your coats and you can wash up at the pump in the kitchen, if you want to."

Yesterday's vegetable soup was long since forgotten, and they were ravenous. They sat around a big old oak table and were served by a generous hand.

At first, too hungry and tired for conversation, they simply ate. Then Dorothy, remembering her manners, said, "We'll never be able to thank you enough for taking in this bunch of refugees."

Nick said heartily, "You ain't refugees, you're family and you'd do the same for us. Have another biscuit."

"What's 'rivergees'?" three-year old Nell asked.

Absently, Burdette said, "Stop kicking the table leg, Nellie."

"You all didn't even act surprised to see us," Ondine observed.

Nick swallowed a mouthful of biscuit and gravy and replied, "I was down to the general store yesterday, and folks was talkin' about the high water in Paducah. I reckoned we'd be seein' you all directly. Sounds like just about everybody in town is havin' to get out. Burdette, honey, have you got any more of them stewed apples?"

The women busied themselves clearing away the breakfast dishes while Burdette tended to her little girls. Water for the dishes came from an old-fashioned hand pump in the kitchen and was heated on the big woodstove. Burdette had made the lye soap herself in a process familiar to all rural families.

Dorothy was the first to be aware of her appearance. Catching sight of her reflection in the wavy kitchen mirror, she was appalled. She looked appraisingly at the others and said, "We're a sight."

It was true. Their shoes and stockings had been soaked with muddy water, dried and soaked again. There had been no opportunity for baths and the men had a two-day growth of whiskers. Their dresses and shirts, already well worn, were wrinkled and limp. Their hair had not been combed since the morning before and their faces were gaunt with fatigue.

Ondine brought in a metal wash tub, pumped water into it and set it on the big woodstove to heat. "We're gonna get cleaned up some. We don't need to look like hobos, even if we are, just about."

She arranged a makeshift screen with an old bed sheet and held out her hands for their dresses and stockings. Taking turns at the tub, they bathed as well as they could, then washed their dresses and stockings and spread them on chairs in front of the woodstove to dry.

"We'll just have to wear our coats today 'til we can iron these," Ondine directed. Dorothy found a comb in her purse and shared it around, a practice she would normally abhor.

Pudgie had fallen asleep, her dark head resting on the table, oblivious to the activity around her.

"Mary War'n, honey, wake up and take off that pinafore so I can wash it," her mother said. "We'll find another place for you to take a nap."

Pudgie asked sleepily, "Did Tom come back?"

"No, but don't worry about Tom. He'll do just fine. Cats can always find something to eat out in the country."

Burdette came in with her toddler, Onie, on her hip, Nell following close on her heels.

"Burdette, I declare," Nannette remarked, "Nell's the spitten' image of you."

Burdette smiled. "Yes, folks do say she favors me some. Why don't we go sit in the front room for awhile, if it's not too cold in there."

Harry, Frank and H.B. were slumped in chairs, nearly asleep. The room felt chilly after the hot kitchen and they were glad of their coats. Ondine volunteered, "We're done in the kitchen, if you all want to go wash. Daddy won't care, if you want to use his razor."

Frank stood up, saying, "I can't say 'no' to that. Come on, Pop, I'll help you first," he said, helping Harry to his feet.

Dorothy went to the window and looked out.

"Burdette, it looks like you're about to have company."

Burdette rose and went to the door. "Good mornin', Ruby May. You're out early of a cold mornin' aren't you?"

A sweet-faced woman peered curiously into the room. "Well, I heard you had some comp'ny and I thought you might could use some extry food. Hidy, Ondine."

Nell had followed her mother to the door. "They ain't comp'ny. They's rivergees."

"Hush, Nellie. Don't say 'ain't'."

"Daddy says it," Nell piped.

Burdette sighed. "Well, you're not to. Run on and play. Come on in, Ruby May, I'm glad to see you," Burdette said, taking a heavy iron pot and skillet from her. "Thank you kindly. That smells like your good ol' beans and cornbread."

Ondine took the iron pot from Burdette, smiling her appreciation. "Hidy, Ruby May. You're mighty good to us. Come in and sit a spell." Burdette introduced the others.

"I hear tell Paducah's got a whole lot of water in it," Ruby May observed.

Louise sat quietly, listening to the easy flow of conversation. She was deeply touched by the Mabry's graciousness and generosity. The Depression had been especially hard on the people in rural areas and she knew that whatever they shared represented sacrifice. The Mabrys had welcomed them all as their own family, sharing their food with them, doing everything possible to help them through a desperate situation.

And now a neighbor, unknown to them, was sharing her food, unsolicited and ungrudging. Dorothy had said, "we'll never be able to thank you enough," but it was more than a polite platitude —it was an absolute truth.

CHAPTER

14

"I think I'll walk down to the general store and see if there's any news out of Paducah," Frank announced. "Anybody else want to go?"

H.B. replied, "Sure, I'll go with you. I need to stretch my legs."

Ondine was ironing her dress, one of a set of four flatirons in her hand. "Don't you all be gone too long. We'll eat supper about four." She turned and set the cooling flatiron back on the wood-stove, replacing it with a heated one.

Frank and H.B. had only been gone a few minutes when the front door opened and they heard Ralph's voice. Eugene was with him. Nannette, looking relieved, said, "Well, look who's here. I was wondering about you."

Ralph looked exhausted. "If I don't ever have to do that again, it'll be okay with me. When we got back to the house, we could hear Pete hollerin', but we couldn't see him, it was so dark. Turned out he'd climbed up on the roof to get out of the water."

Eugene added, "We finally got him into the boat, but he almost took a dunkin' doin' it," he guffawed.

"I'll bet it wouldn't've been so funny if it had been you, Eugene Mabry," Ondine chided him.

"Burdette, if you all ever do get electricity out here, make Daddy buy you an electric iron."

Turning back to Eugene, she said, "You're just foolin', aren't you? The water's not really that high, is it?"

Eugene shook his head. "We're not foolin'."

Dorothy came into the kitchen. "How did you all get out here?" she asked.

"We rowed that ol' boat on back to 30th and Broadway. Then we hitched a ride from there some of the way and the rest of the way we walked," Eugene explained.

"Where's Pete?" Ondine inquired. "He said he'd just stay out there at the drugstore 'til daylight. I've gotta go back, but maybe I can get a ride over to Bardwell to see Sammie Jane and the kids first."

The front door opened again, this time to admit Nick, home from his day's work. Nell and Patsy were engaged in a noisy custody dispute over a Shirley Temple doll as Onie looked on with detached interest.

Louise was mortified. "No, no, Patsy, that's Nell's dolly." She picked her daughter up, Patsy protesting strongly.

"Aw, now Louise, I wanta see which one of them little heatherns wins," Nick said, laughing.

A large pot of savory stew simmered on the woodstove alongside Ruby May's beans. Burdette moved around her kitchen serenely, unruffled by the crowd of people thronging her house. Never once did her hospitality waver.

Over supper, Nick offered, "I stopped by the General Store on the way home and somebody said there's a cow up on a second-floor porch in Paducah."

"Well, I'll be!" Frank mused. "I guess Aunt Ider's not crazy after all."

When supper was over, Burdette and Ondine set about making sleeping arrangements for a houseful of people. An early rising means an early bedtime. The house, never spacious, was now bursting at the seams. It meant sleeping three to a bed, sleeping in chairs, sleeping on the floor. A bureau drawer was emptied to provide a crib for Patsy.

The wind rose during the night and January found its way under doors and around windows.

The next morning, they were up early again. Burdette was back in her kitchen preparing their customary hearty breakfast before Nick left on his route. When breakfast was over and the dishes were washed, it would still be almost two hours before full daylight. When dawn broke, they looked out to see that a fresh layer of snow had fallen overnight.

Later that day, Eugene came in. "I got to talkin' to Sammie Jane and she says why don't some of y'all come stay with us? We've got room and she'd like the company, what with me bein' gone all the time."

After some discussion, it was decided that Dorothy and Harry would remain in Cunningham with Ondine and Frank, and all the others would go with Eugene to Bardwell.

The little house in Bardwell was only slightly larger than the house in Cunningham, but Sammie Jane made them feel welcome. She and Eugene had two little girls, the elder almost exactly Patsy's age. Louise asked if she could hold the baby, Jane Ross.

"Oh, isn't she the sweetest little thing," Louise exclaimed. "And Alma Jean is a little doll."

Sammie Jane smiled. "Yes, they're pretty good little girls most of the time. Eugene's been telling me about the flood. That's such a shame. I don't know what I'd do if I had to pick up and leave everything like that, but I guess if you know you have to do it, you just do it."

H.B. had walked out to the mailbox and he came back with a spring in his step. He gave Sammie Jane her mail and drew Louise aside. "When I was out at the mailbox, I got to talking to one of the neighbors and he told me he's going to drive to Mayfield tomorrow. I told him that I have folks there and he said we could ride with him if we want to. What do you think?"

Louise hesitated for a second, then said, "Oh…well…that sounds like a good idea. But where would we stay?"

H.B. had several close relatives who lived in or near Mayfield and she knew he thought his family would be there. "I thought we'd go to Uncle Sam and Aunt Etta in Hickory or we could go to Uncle Clayton and Aunt Estelle."

Louise paused. "They won't know to expect us though. What if we can't stay with them?"

H.B. replied, "I think they're probably wondering where we are."

CHAPTER

15

When Horace's half-brother, Sam Hargrove, was a young man, someone asked him, "Sam, when are you gonna get married?" He replied, "When I can find a girl like Bess."

So he married Bess's younger sister, Etta Wright, making the children of both unions "double cousins," or as Mary Lee more precisely phrased it "one and three-quarter cousins." Sam was a dairy farmer with a house-to-house delivery service of his dairy products. His farm was in Graves County a few miles north of Mayfield, the county seat.

Etta was sweeping the front porch when she heard the sound of a car coming up the road that ran in front of their farmhouse. She didn't recognize the car so was surprised when it came to a stop in front of their property, still more surprised when H.B., Louise and Patsy got out.

"Land's sake, H.B., we've been wonderin' about you all ever since we heard about the flood." She greeted Louise cordially and patted Patsy.

H.B. said, "I thought maybe Mom and Dad and the kids would be here."

"Why, no, they're not here. We haven't heard anything from them since Bess's last letter two weeks ago. Wesley and Opal were here yesterday, and they haven't heard from them either. If they were at Clayton's, or at George and Minnie's, we'd know about it. Now, where do you s'pose they've got off to?"

Perplexed, H.B. shook his head.

"Well, now, come on in the house and get warm and I'll make us some coffee. This is bakin' day and I've got some bread set to rise so I need to go see about it. Just take off your coats and have a seat."

Going to her kitchen, Etta punched down her bread dough in the big earthenware bowl, turned it, covered it and set it in a warm place for its second rising. She filled a big spatter ware coffee pot and set it on the stove to brew, then returned to her visitors.

H.B. described conditions in Paducah and told about being forced out of their home.

"My lands. What're folks going to do? I never thought the river would get that high. I wish Horace hadn't moved you all up there to Paducah. Still, a man has to go where his work is."

H.B. cleared his throat. "Aunt Etta, the fact is, we need a place to stay. Do you think you and Uncle Sam could put us up for awhile?"

"Why, H.B., you know you all are welcome to stay with us. Sam's out in the barn, but he ought to be comin' in to eat after awhile and I'll talk to him about it. He'll be glad to see you all."

"How long do you figure on stayin'?" Sam asked in his direct way.

H.B. replied, "We don't know. We didn't think it would be a real big flood, anyway no worse than in 1913, but the water doesn't show any signs of going down yet. For all we know, our house and everything in it is flooded. We'll help out around here every way we can to earn our keep."

Sam thought for a minute. "Well, now, you'll be welcome

to stay three, four days but we can't afford to keep you all longer than that. Ruth's married and gone but we've still got Billy and Julia and Lucille at home. I reckon Clayton and Estelle can take you for awhile after that."

Louise had dusted the furniture and was running a carpet sweeper over the parlor rug. When she had asked Aunt Etta how she could help, she had replied, "Louise, I'm so used to doing things my own way I don't know how to have help. Julia and Lucille have their chores and Billy helps his daddy. If you want to, you can clean the parlor a little bit." Louise made quick work of it, emptied the carpet sweeper and returned it to the pantry.

Etta sat down at the kitchen table with her work basket. "Louise, how would you like to cut out some quilt pieces for me?"

"Oh, yes, I can do that. What kind of quilt are you making?"

"It'll be a Lone Star when it's done. My sister-in-law, Minnie, just finished one and it's the prettiest quilt I've ever seen." She gave Louise a bag of quilt scraps, a pair of scissors and a piece of cardboard cut in a diamond shape.

"See this blue calico with the little red figure in it? I bought the goods from a peddler that came to my Mama and Daddy's house before I married Sam. Daddy thought I gave too much money for it, but it made a right pretty dress. I got a lot of good out of it when I was teaching school."

Louise paused in her cutting and looked up. "I didn't know you were a school teacher."

Etta laid out several quilt pieces on the table, arranging and rearranging them until the combination of colors and patterns pleased her. She threaded her needle and began to stitch them together.

"Yes, I taught eight grades in a one-room schoolhouse. I liked it just fine and I reckon I would have kept on at it my whole life if I hadn't married Sam Hargrove. Daddy wanted Bess to be a teacher, too. She was smart and she would have made a good teacher but she was scared of some of the big boys and she thought they wouldn't mind her and that they'd make her cry." Etta laughed. "They didn't want to mind me, either, and they did try to make me cry but I can tell you they didn't try it but once! Here's a piece from a dress Bess wore to a barn dance, and a piece from Mama's favorite dress. And these were from little dresses that Ruth and Julia and Lucille wore. H-m-m. These scraps bring back a lot of memories."

Louise was quiet for a minute. Then she said, "My mother was working on a Rose of Sharon quilt just a week before she passed away."

"How much had she gotten done on it?" Etta asked.

"She'd finished the top, but she'd just started quilting it."

"Do you s'pose you'll finish it?"

"Maybe, someday. I've been working on a flower garden quilt top. I just hope the river hasn't gotten it." Louise felt the need to change the subject. "Tell me some more about when you taught school."

"Why, I taught out of the *McGuffey's Readers*. Most of the pupils were under fourteen years old. Back then, as soon as a child could read and write and do a little bit of arithmetic, a lot of their folks thought they'd learned enough and took them out of school to help at home. An eighth grade education was pretty good in those days but not too many stayed that long. I always enjoyed teaching the little ones the most. The bigger they got the more they thought they knew more than I did."

She grew quiet and the two women worked on in a companionable silence. Louise was glad they had come. She had known Aunt Etta ever since she and H.B. married, but she hadn't been well acquainted with her. She found she liked her very much.

After a while, Etta put her work away and stood up. "Sam and H.B. and Billy will be wantin' their lunch before long."

The quiet of the house was broken when Julia and Lucille came home from school. Julia was eighteen years old, serious and quiet. Lucille was fourteen, a perky blue-eyed blonde.

Etta said, "Lucille, you can thank Louise for cleaning the parlor for you. You can help me in the kitchen now."

"Thanks, Louise. Mama, I've got a lot of homework and Bobby Martin's coming over to help me."

Julia mimicked, " 'Bobby Martin's coming over to help me'...if you ask me, he's the one who needs the help."

Etta handed Lucille a pan of potatoes to be peeled and wordlessly pointed to the kitchen table.

Louise said, "I'll be glad to peel those pota —" but broke off when Etta smiled slightly and shook her head. Lucille flounced to the table, sat down and picked up a paring knife, fuming.

"Julia, you can go see if the hens have laid," Etta directed.

As they got ready for bed that night, H.B. said, "One thing about dairy farming, you never run out of something to do. I'm worn out! How was your day?"

Louise replied, "It was nice, but I'm afraid I wasn't much

help. Aunt Etta didn't find much for me to do, but I had a good visit with her. I got a kick out of the girls. Sisters are pretty much alike everywhere, I guess."

At the end of the week, they got into Sam's old Ford to go to Uncle Clayton's farm on Pryorsburg Road. Aunt Etta went out to the car with them, handing Louise a pie covered with a napkin.

"This is Estelle's pie dish and it would be bad manners to send it back to her empty. They always like my caramel pie." She waved to them as the car pulled away, calling, "When you find out where Horace and Bess are, be sure to let us know."

CHAPTER 16

Aunt Estelle came out to welcome them. "We were hopin' you all would come stay with us. You're just as welcome as you can be. I was a little bit jealous because you went to Sam and Etta first," she said, laughing. She held out her arms to Patsy, who went to her without hesitating. "You all come on in the house and get warm. My sakes, it looks like it's fixin' to snow again. Sam, why didn't Etta come with you? Clayton's out feedin' the stock. Go out and tell him to come in and see his nephew and his family and we'll have some pie."

Aunt Estelle was a non-stop talker, good-natured and generous. She led them into the spotless house straight through to the big kitchen. Clayton came in through the back door, smiling broadly. He shook hands with H.B. and gave Louise a bashful grin. "I thought maybe Horace and Bess would come, too."

Louise told them about the telephone call. "I guess they meant to tell us where they were going but I never did find out."

Clayton reassured them, "There's a lot of places they might've gone. Don't fret, they'll turn up."

Day followed day, until a week had passed since they had left their home. H.B. had learned that all evacuees were ordered to go to the basement of the Graves County Court House in Mayfield's town square to receive typhoid shots. Patsy became sick, feverish and cranky following the inoculations.

At the courthouse, H.B. met Leo Dudley, a Mayfield businessman. Mr. Dudley was concerned about the plight of all the Paducah citizens who had descended on Mayfield.

"Why, say, H.B., I've got some business in Lone Oak tomorrow and if you want to ride along with me we can go on to Paducah and maybe you can find out something about your house." H.B. seized the opportunity and was ready right after lunch.

When Mr. Dudley had completed his business, he said, "All right, now let's go see about Paducah." He was able to obtain the use of a motorboat at the evacuation point, by now all but deserted.

When they had left Paducah, darkness had obscured the full extent of the flooding. Now, in full daylight, H.B.was shocked by the enormity of the disaster. The river that had always looked so beautiful and benign had reached out and claimed the little city.

They had reached 21st and Kentucky Avenue when the motor choked, sputtered and stopped. Mr. Dudley said mildly, "Well, shoot, now." He tried repeatedly to get it started again, finally accepting that it had just quit. "I reckon we'll have to row the rest of the way," he said with resignation. Lifting the oars, they dipped them into the water and pulled hard, realizing right away that they were rowing against a strong current.

After what seemed a long time, H.B. saw the swamped filling station at the corner of 19th and Kentucky Avenue. His arms and shoulders were aching. Mr. Dudley let his oar rest in the holder while he fumbled in his pocket for his pipe and tobacco pouch. When he had filled and lit it, the boat had already drifted back several feet.

"Well, H.B., what do you say? Do you want to keep goin'? I don't want to let you down, but no better time than we're makin', I don't think we can make it to South 4th Street and back out to

1937 flood. Old Market House and south 2nd Street in distance.

1937 flood. 4th and Broadway.

1937 Flood. Old Post Office and Palmer Hotel at 5th and Broadway.

the end of Broadway before it gets dark."

H.B. replied, "I was thinking the same thing. We don't want to be out here on the water after dark. Anyhow I reckon I don't need to see the house now to know what's happened to it."

"Oh, that's pretty material," Louise exclaimed. "What are you making?"

Estelle held her work up and showed Louise that it was a little dress. "I've been savin' this feed sack for a long time. I thought it was a pretty piece of goods, 'way too pretty for an apron, but it's just right for a little girl's dress."

Louise was delighted. "Oh, Aunt Estelle —oh, and you've even smocked it."

Estelle smiled. "I always wanted a little girl so I could dress her up all cute. I told Bess one time, I said, 'Bess, I don't think it's fair. The Lord sent you all kinds of babies, a boy and a girl with yellow hair and blue eyes and a boy and a girl with black hair and brown eyes, but He just sent me all one kind, six big ol' black-haired, brown-eyed boys'." Her laugh told Louise that she wouldn't have traded any one of those boys for a dozen little girls.

"And besides," she continued, "I don't think that little dress Patsy's been wearin' will stand much more washin'. Look in my button box and see if you can find me three little white buttons that kind of match."

Lack of communication added much to the stress and anxiety of the situation, so they listened to the radio at every opportunity. National newscasts carried frequent stories and updates on the crisis..."**over 10,500 driven from their homes in the Ohio Valley**"..."**living in boxcars and schoolhouses**"..."**Red Cross has set up a relief body**"..."**mandatory evacuation in Paducah, Kentucky**"..."**river expected to peak by the middle of next week**"..."**20,000 homeless in Paducah...**"

Newsman Lowell Thomas spoke particularly of Paducah's plight. The airways carried personal messages from people all over the United States hoping to learn the location of their loved ones. One evening after supper, the family sat listening to the old Atwater-Kent radio when Louise sat bolt upright with excitement.

"Oh, did you all hear that? My brother, Harry —oh, bless his heart, he must be so worried. I have to write to him right now. Aunt Estelle, may I please borrow some paper and an envelope and...and a stamp?"

Estelle chuckled. "Honey, you don't have to borrow. I think we can spare 'em just fine."

Late the next afternoon, H.B. had just come in from helping Clayton in the barn when he heard a familiar voice. His heart skipped when his brother Dick appeared in the doorway.

"Hi, Aitch," he said, grinning. It was a moment before H.B. could find his voice.

"Dick, where in time have you all been? Where are Mom and Dad and Mary?"

"Simmer down, Aitch. We've been stayin' with Aunt Fanny out in Lone Oak. Mom and Dad and Mary are still there and Louise Mac and Jimmy are there now, too. It was gettin' pretty crowded and when Aunt Cordelia showed up, I decided to scram. I hitched a ride to Mayfield and then just walked on out here."

H.B. laughed at the mention of Aunt Cordelia. "Yeah, I reckon I'd've scrammed, too. How come Louise Mac and Jimmy are here?"

"They say that Louisville's flooded pretty bad, too. The Corps of Engineers was gonna send J.B. off somewhere, so he put Louise and Jimmy on a train to come down here. They had to take the L.&N., though, and they took a bus from Nashville to Lone Oak. The I.C. can't get through Paducah because of the flood."

Relief had washed over H.B. as he was assured that all his family were safe and well. He had been so sure that they would have gone to Mayfield that he had forgotten about Horace's step-sister, Fanny Drinkard Wood. They had sensibly gone to the nearest place of refuge.

Ruefully, H.B. said, "I was in Lone Oak with Leo Dudley

the other day. If I'd known you all were there, I'd've come to see you."

Dick inquired, "What were you doin' in Lone Oak?" H.B. explained his failed attempt to check on the house.

"Sounds pretty bad, Aitch. I reckon our house won't be any better off."

"Say, how'd you know we were out here?" H.B. asked.

"I saw Billy down at the courthouse square and he told me. You reckon Aunt Estelle will put me up for awhile? I don't want to go back to Aunt Fanny's house 'til Aunt Cordelia gets on her broom and flies back where she came from."

CHAPTER 17

On February 2, 1937, the Ohio River crested at 60.2 feet, giving it a breadth of seven miles at its widest point. Nobody had ever imagined that a flood of that magnitude was possible.

On February 14th, it was announced on the radio that the streets of Paducah were clear. It had been twenty-three days since H.B. and Louise left their home.

H.B. made plans to return to Paducah, leaving Louise and Patsy in Clayton and Estelle's care until he could determine what living conditions he would encounter. He borrowed two dollars from Clayton and got a ride back to Paducah, his spirits rising as he came closer to the little city and counted off the familiar landmarks.

Nothing could have prepared him for what he was about to see.

He was met with a scene of almost unbelievable destruction. Downtown, almost every store window had been broken. Everywhere he looked, everything was covered with mud and filth. A stench, so vile that he found it hard to breathe, filled the air. Clean-up efforts were underway, but the streets and sidewalks were still strewn with wreckage.

He walked to the little house at 502 South 4th Street. The front steps felt weak under his weight. He looked in the front window, then tried to open the door. It was firmly stuck so he turned away. From what he had seen, he really didn't want to go inside anyway. He wondered how he could tell Louise what he had found.

He walked back to town, went to the Arcade and found it in ruins. Going back to his sign shop, he found his big easel lying top down, its boards sprung apart. The trolley that had held his paints was overturned and falling to pieces; the cans of paint and his brushes, pencils, compass, lettering pens, India ink, and yard-sticks were nowhere to be found. Only the big shears remained, and they lay rusting in the ruins of the easel. All of the equipment that had provided a living for him and his family was gone.

He did, however, find work of a sort. Someone had had the foresight to remove all the cushions from the theatre seats, storing them in the balconies. The interior of the Arcade was being hosed down and shoveled out and H.B. was hired to retrieve the seat cushions and backs and reattach them to their frames. He made trip after trip up and down the balcony stairs, balancing the cushions and backs in his arms, then fitting them to their frames, bolting each one in place. For this, he was paid twenty-five cents an hour.

Someone suggested that he might find a place to sleep on the mezzanine at Kresge's. Sure enough, he found a broken-down sofa there, moldy and damp-smelling, but big enough to stretch out on it. A moth-eaten army blanket that looked as if it had seen service in the Great War was folded at one end.

He woke during the night with a stinging at the back of his throat. By morning, he had a heavy cold. Trying to shake off the miserable feeling, he returned to the Arcade and went on with his work of replacing the seat cushions. When that job was completed, he went to the Columbia to continue the process of restoring the theatres to a useable condition.

The aftermath.

In the days that followed, more and more people returned to Paducah, wondering if the town they loved could ever be restored. Houses had to be hosed down, ceilings, walls and floors. Furniture had been destroyed, books and pictures ruined, curtains and draperies unfit even to wash. Plastered walls crumbled, floors buckled. People who had been fortunate enough to own pianos could only take what remained of them and consign them to Guthrie Pit, a hollow in the vicinity of South 16th Street. And over it all, that foul odor permeated everything.

H.B. worked every day, sleeping on the old sofa, eating when and where he could, saving every penny that he could. A barber shop near the Market House offered a bath in a clean-scrubbed tub with a bar of soap and a fresh white towel for twenty-five cents.

He went back to his shop to make a start on cleaning it up and was surprised to find Frank there. "How's it goin'?" he asked.

Frank managed a tired grin, shook his head and said, "Probably about the same way it's goin' for everybody else. Ralph and I came on back to town to see about our houses. Ondine and

The aftermath.

Dorothy are still out at Cunningham and Nannette's helping Sammie Jane with the kids at Bardwell. We decided to work on Dad's house and try to get it fit to live in so they'll have a place to stay while we try to do something about our own. We put Dad on a train to New York to go stay with Harry and Matt, and Ralph and Nannette sent Mary War'n to stay with Nannette's folks. When's Louise coming back?" Without waiting for an answer, he went on, "If she wants to come on back home, you all could stay out at Dad's house with the rest of us."

Suddenly, H.B.'s world looked brighter. He bought a penny postcard at the post office and wrote to Louise, telling her about Frank's suggestion. He asked her to write to him, addressing her letter to him at General Delivery.

He missed his family, he missed his home. He wanted life to return to normal.

The next day, he went out to Harry's house to help make preparations. He found the doors and windows all standing open, admitting fresh air and beginning to dry the penetrating damp. The

The aftermath.

wallpaper, already falling off, had been stripped completely, leaving the walls mottled, cracked and mildewed. The floor had buckled. The few pieces of furniture that had survived had been moved out into the back yard. The mattresses had all been sent to Guthrie Pit and the bedsprings leaned against the back of the house, having been thoroughly hosed down and scrubbed with a stiff brush. The curtains had been stripped from the windows and thrown away. Trash wagons passed by often, piled high with ruined household goods, accepting even more.

He wondered if he had been wrong to ask Louise to come back home.

CHAPTER 18

A week later, Louise and Patsy returned to Paducah. Louise was horrified by conditions in the city, not realizing the improvements that had been achieved in a couple of weeks. She was recovering from an attack of flu so they went directly out to Harry's house.

New mattresses had been purchased on credit and with Ondine, Dorothy and Nannette's efforts, a new household was beginning to take shape. Nannette and Ralph, Ondine and Frank soon returned to their respective homes to begin the process of making them livable again.

H.B. dreaded taking Louise back to see their house but knew it couldn't be postponed indefinitely. There had been no opportunity to begin cleaning and it was still just as he had seen it when he first returned to Paducah. At last, Louise insisted on going back to see it.

Leaving Patsy in Dorothy's care, they rode a bus to town. They walked the four blocks down South 4th Street. The house was almost unrecognizable. The neatly painted little duplex stood mud-stained to the tops of the windows. They walked up the weakened front steps and H.B. tried again to open the door.

"It wouldn't open the first time I tried it but I thought it was just swollen. I'll go around and try the back door." He walked through the side yard, remembering that last day when he had gone after the coal. The ground was still soft but not muddy now.

He tried the back door and was able to push it open a few inches. When he entered the house, he took a minute to look around him. His impulse was to leave at once and take Louise away without seeing it but he knew her too well to think she would accept that.

He made his way to the front door and saw that the buckled floor was keeping the door from opening. Going out again through the back door, he went around to the front of the house.

"Hon, I guess you'll have to come in through the back door. The front door's not going to open. Louise, are you sure you want to go inside?"

Without answering, she joined him and they walked through the side yard together. She paused for a moment. "Look, Pill, the lilac bush already has some little buds on it. It's early this year, isn't it?"

Together, they went up the back steps and entered the house. Louise said nothing. Everything was covered with mud and filth. The linoleum on the kitchen floor was completely hidden by a layer of silt. The kitchen table had collapsed and parts of the chairs had floated into the bedroom. Their efforts to put their furniture out of harm's way had come to nothing.

Something had clogged the drain of the claw-foot bathtub and it brimmed with filthy floodwater. The bathmat lay on the floor, a moldy mass.

The new wallpaper was stained and distempered, coming off in strips. The pretty flowered curtains that Louise had sewn so carefully hung brown and limp at the windows, clotted with mud, mildewed. The secretary had fallen over and was coming apart.

H.B. turned when he heard Louise begin to cry. She was kneeling on the floor trying to rub the mud off of a warped wooden board. He went closer and he could see, defined by the imbedded mud, a deep, curved scratch. It was all that was recognizable of the dining table.

He stood helplessly, wanting to comfort her but not knowing what to say.

He turned and went over to the mantle. The copy of *Anthony Adverse* was on top of the stacked books and was unharmed. He picked it up and tucked it under his arm.

Except for some dishes, there was almost nothing salvageable in the house but, unexplainably, the sewing machine had somehow survived.

At last, Louise got to her feet. "Let's go," she said.

They reached the bus-stop but wordlessly agreed to continue walking back to the house on Madison Street. Louise struggled to regain her composure but the tears wouldn't stop.

At last, H.B. ventured, "You know, Hon, we'll get through this. We'll just have to start over, that's all. Lots of other people are having to do the same thing."

"I know it," Louise choked out. "But H. B., where will we ever find the money to start over again? We have nothing left, nothing at all."

H.B.replied, "Well, Hon, when you stop to think about it, we didn't have anything when we started out but we were managing okay. My work is already starting to pick up with people trying to get their businesses going again and needing signs. It'll probably take a while, but we'll be okay."

She slipped her arm through his. Drawing a deep, quivering breath she said, "Yes…we'll be okay."

CHAPTER

19

Ralph and Nannette were among the many who had to start over. The new dry-cleaning plant had been badly damaged by the flood, the equipment ruined. They worked diligently to get the plant restored and ready to resume operations in as short a time as possible. Consequently, they were there most of their waking hours.

"As long as we're in the neighborhood, let's stop by to see Nannette and Ralph," Louise suggested. H.B. had painted some signs for a grocery store on North 13th Street and she had walked with him to deliver them.

They were surprised to find Ondine, Frank and Dorothy there. Dorothy was visibly upset. Ralph grinned. "What is this, a family reunion?"

Frank and Ondine seemed both apprehensive and excited. "You might as well tell them your news, too," Nannette said. Dorothy began to cry.

"Well, we've decided to move to California. Uncle John wrote and told me about a place in Alhambra that's hirin'. We've been talkin' about it for awhile and it just feels like the time is right."

"But it's so far away," Dorothy protested through her tears. "I never dreamed you'd do such a thing. There's Harry 'way out on the east coast and we almost never get to see him. Now, here you are, going off in the opposite direction, only a lot farther!"

"Okay, Dorothy, I didn't say we were goin' tomorrow,"

Frank said. "We'll be here a few more weeks. Once we get settled, you can come visit us if you want to."

Ondine added, "We hope everybody'll come, maybe even move out there with us."

Louise said nothing. California. He might as well have said they were moving to Mars. She felt as if she wanted to cry, too.

H.B. asked, practically, "Are you sure of the job? That'd be a long way to go to get out there and not have work."

"Uncle John knows the people, and he's pretty certain they'll take me on. He says he'll look out for a job for Ondine, too."

Mention of Uncle John made Louise feel a little better. He was their mother's older brother, well-loved by all the family. He and Aunt Florence had lived in California for a long time.

Ralph said, "Well, good luck —I mean it. You're probably doin' the best thing."

Dorothy wept anew. She had hoped Ralph would talk them out of it.

Later that day, the shop door opened and Nick Mabry came in carrying a large cardboard carton that appeared to have a life of its own. "Nannette, I'm bringin' your cat back, safe and sound. I like to've never caught it, but here it is, no worse for wear. I'm sorry I can't say the same for the dogs out my way, though. This ol' cat's whupped every dog in Carlisle County."

Horace and Bess

CHAPTER 20

"Horace, why don't you take Jimmy and Patsy out to the porch swing?" Bess suggested. The two children had been competing to see which one could make the most noise and even Bess's almost endless patience with her grandchildren was wearing thin.

Louise Mac said, "I don't know but what you'd do better to just move to another house, Mother. It's going to take so much work to make this house fit to live in again."

Bess replied, "Almost every house in Paducah is in as bad shape or worse. We're used to this house so I expect we'll stay here awhile longer. The landlord says he'll have somebody over tomorrow to paint and put up new wallpaper."

"What are you going to do about furniture?" Louise Mac inquired. They had scrubbed the house inside and out; what remained of their furniture stood at the curb, waiting to be taken to Guthrie Pit.

"We'll buy what we just have to have," Bess replied. "Cousin Lily says we can have Aunt Briggs' old bed and dresser if we'll come and get it."

Mary Lee had been listening, but now protested. "But Mama, that stuff is so old-fashioned and ugly. That awful old bed looks like that picture of the one Abraham Lincoln died in. Why can't we buy some of that nice red maple furniture instead?"

"We'll need more than just the one bed and dresser, so we'll see about one suite of the red maple if it's not too high. Dick won't mind sleeping on a sofa-davenport, so that'll be enough to get us by for awhile. Come to think of it, though, we'll have to have a table and some chairs and a kitchen cabinet, too. H.B. says he'll come over Saturday and he and Horace and Dick can go over to Uncle Joe's house to get the bed and dresser. H.B. knows somebody with a wagon who'll help 'em bring it over. I think it was mighty good of Cousin Lily to offer it. It won't matter that it's old and not very pretty."

Changing the subject, Mary Lee said, "Mama, when H.B. and Louise D. get back, don't forget to show 'em that letter and newspaper clipping from Aunt Ida."

Patsy and Jimmy had subsided and were sitting with their grandfather in the porch swing, listening as he sang *Swing Low, Sweet Chariot*. They were an appreciative audience. Their good behavior was short-lived, however. When Patsy saw her parents crossing the street and walking toward the house, she climbed down from the swing, jumping up and down and shrieking at the top of her voice. Not to be outdone, Jimmy joined in. Louise and H.B. shushed them, laughing.

"Did you find anything?" Bess wanted to know. Louise had declared that she couldn't face going back to live in their old house again, so they were looking for new living quarters.

"We looked at three different places and they're all in pretty bad shape. We've just about decided to take a duplex about a block from here though," H.B. replied. "It's the best we've found and the landlord's working on it right now. If we take it we can move in next week."

Mary Lee emerged from the house holding Bess's handbag. "Mama, don't forget..."

Bess laughed self-consciously. "You're not going to let me forget, are you?" She took an envelope from her handbag and handed it to H.B. "I got a letter from Ida yesterday with this newspaper clipping in it."

H.B. and Louise seated themselves on the front steps and

H.B. began to read.

Riverside, California—

LETTER TO RIVERSIDER
FROM A
KENTUCKY RELATIVE
TELLS OF FLOOD
EPISODES

A letter received here by Mrs. F. E. Maddocks of 3315 Third Street from her sister, Mrs. H.B.Hargrove, a resident of Paducah, Ky., but written from Mayfield, the present temporary residence of her family, gives an intimate picture of conditions there as a result of the unprecedented floods of the Ohio and Mississippi Rivers.

"We are among the first to leave Paducah," said Mrs. Hargrove, writing under date of Jan. 31. "We fixed up our household goods the best we could the 22nd and got a taxi to take us to Horace's step-sister's house in Lone Oak (a suburb). The water was running very fast. It was so high the taxi couldn't get us in front of the house but had to drive back in the alley.

"We drove through water so deep that it ran over the floor of the car, and it was pouring sleet so hard the driver could hardly see his way.

"We have been out nine days and the water is still rising but not near so fast. We have seen two of our neighbors who were on second floors who said that the water was nearly to the roof over our front porch when they left the middle of last week; so everything we have is deep in that water and will be for a long time. The river will be about eight feet higher than ever before.

"This is the only disastrous flood that Paducah has ever had, and it was not thought possible. Paducah is being completely evacuated. People can't even stay in their rooms which are above the waters on account of the water supply being cut off and the sewerage system being ruined.

"We had three nice suites of furniture, practically new. We bought our dining room suite on the 14th day of December. We brought out a good many of our clothes and two good suit cases and two blankets. That's all we have outside of that water. We have been very fortunate and will never realize what many people have suffered.

"We were so sorry to hear of the freezing weather in California. 12 above has been our lowest temperature and that only once. Every school in West Kentucky is closed to use the buses to bring people out of Paducah and the buildings to house them.

"They say it will be a month at least before people can go back to Paducah."

Jimmy and Patsy

H.B. looked at his mother with admiration. "Well, what do you know about that? Our mother has had a letter published in a California newspaper! That was a really good article, Mom."

Bess's cheeks went pink. "Oh," she demurred, "anybody can write a letter."

CHAPTER 21

Spring came at last. The first green spears of daffodils pushed through the soft earth. The trees took on their familiar blush before the leaves appeared on their branches and the birds sang as if nothing bad had ever happened or ever would.

H.B. and Louise had moved into a brick duplex at 9th and Adams Street. Louise had worked hard to make a comfortable home with the few pieces of second-hand furniture they had acquired. They made the final payment on the ill-fated dining room suite and began to talk of buying a few essential new pieces.

Gradually, ordinary life returned to Paducah. There was talk of a floodwall being built to prevent another such disaster. A few people objected, complaining that the wall would block the beautiful view. Others squelched them promptly, saying that losing their homes and belongings was too high a price to pay for a view, no matter how beautiful.

And spring melted into summer.

On a hot July evening, H.B. came home from work, whistling two notes as he came through the door. Louise whistled back —or tried to. He found her in the kitchen starting supper. "Have you had a nice day?" she asked as he kissed her.

"Pretty fair, I reckon. Something sure smells good. What have you and Patsy been doing today?"

"Oh, well, I made some tomato relish and put up eight pints of it. Then we went downtown and paid the light bill. Patsy's getting so she doesn't like the stroller much anymore. She kept wanting to climb out and walk."

H.B. grinned. "Sounds like she's about to get too big for her britches. Did we get any mail?"

Louise hesitated for a second. "Oh —well —we got a letter from Harry. Want to read it?"

H.B. poured himself a glass of cold water from the bottle in the icebox. "Why don't you read it to me while I cool off?"

"Well —I'd really rather you read it."

He glanced at her quizzically as he began to read Harry's angular handwriting.

"Dad's all right, but he misses you...the boys are growing up fast...weather's hot, even for New York... lean times in Paducah...come stay with us...plenty of room...job opportunities in the field of commercial art...I know people H.B. could contact...advantages in a big city...Matt sends her love..."

H.B. set the empty water glass down on the table. They looked at each other for a long moment.

"What do you think?" H.B. asked.

But that's another story.

H.B. Hargrove, Jr.

EPILOGUE

U ncle Harry's invitation was too good to pass up. Bolstered by Frank and Ondine's courageous move across country to California, after much discussion, they decided to try their luck in New York City. In August, 1937, Uncle Harry drove all the way to Paducah to take us back with him (Aunt Dot, too) to his home at 3919 53rd Street, Woodside, Long Island, New York.

As a child not yet three years old, I have no memories at all of the events that took place there. My grandparents kept the letters that my parents wrote, painting a word-picture of a huge city as seen through the eyes of a young Kentucky couple and describing their hopes and, ultimately, their disillusionment.

August 25, 1937

Dearest Folks,
We arrived in N. Y. yesterday pretty tired however we did have a beautiful trip.
The first stretch of the trip took us just fourteen miles outside Richmond, Ind. which is a beautiful place also much larger than I thought, has some pretty big buildings.
We spent the nite in a tourist camp and were so sleepy we really turned in early. The little cabins were so nice and clean.
Next morning we left about six and drove all day till about six and found another camp on summit of Mount Laurel at 2601 ft. The little cabin was of log and the camp was called "Sunset Inn" it really was a beautiful place but turned awfully cold. We each had to use two pairs of double blankets. We were so anxious to take snaps but next morning was raining. We did take couple but don't know if they will be good or not. Hope they will be so we can send you some.
The next morning while eating breakfast the owner came in and

wanted to know where the little girl was and he had a pet ground hog. He made it sit up and gave it a small piece of candy and the little thing sat there and held it with his little paws and just smacked his lips over it. We nearly had a fit over it, said he had already made his bed for the winter under the big cabin.

We left there about seven and had more mountains also passed snake farms. When we drove through Maryland over mountains were even larger at one point the height was 3073 called "Backbone Mountains" and for some time drove through clouds some very heavy ones we couldn't see much of the scenery but that in itself was an experience.

The Skyline drive in the Blue Ridge Mts was lovely not quite so large as others at 1150 ft.

Oh, we went through so many interesting places it would be difficult to tell all.

We had an experience in Pa. We were riding along eating sand-wiches enjoying scenery and not noticing how fast we were going when all at once a speed cop drove up beside us and began asking questions. Well we were all lovely to him and he just told us to slow down, but it certainly made a very careful bunch from then on.

Tuesday we arrived in Va. about three and stayed there till next morning. Mat has a sister living there. She decided to take us over to see Washington that is to see the main points of interest in just a short time that is really a beautiful city doesn't seem to have the noise and confusion N.Y. has.

H.B.has already been in the N. Y. business section twice once last nite and again today, went down with Jack and Bill who were delighted to show him about. I haven't been down yet.

Mat, Dorothy and I went down to a neighborhood business section this afternoon but that isn't much to see.

This is a mighty big city for a little country gal, I didn't

Pages 5 and 6 are missing but take up on page 7 in Dad's (H. B.'s) handwriting:

....of the route we took—
We crossed the Ohio River Sunday at Evansville, Ind. (We saw only the suburbs of this town, but the minute we had crossed the

river, the difference in the country became noticeable—the towns and farms alike were much better kept and more prosperous than in West Ky. We went north to Terre Haute, Ind. where we ran into rain—and an American Legion Convention which caused us to detour around the outskirts. Our route then carried us through the heart of Indianapolis an interesting and busy place a little larger than Louisville. Just before we crossed the line into Ohio, we passed through Richmond, Ind.—a place slightly smaller than Paducah, but with a business section twice as large and much more "citified". About 6 pm Sunday we entered Ohio and spent the night At Mac-Donalds Camp as pictured on the card. The next morning we passed through Springfield and saw the main plant of the Crowell Publishing Co. After that through the capital city—Columbus where we saw some really beautiful and tall buildings. By this time the weather was really cool and I had no coat so we stopped and I bought a sweater at Montgomery Wards. The store was a big one, covering half a block and having 4 floors and a basement. About noon Monday we passed thru Zanesville, a big pottery town, but rather old and ugly. It was there that we began to get into the hills and the scenery was grand. For about 40 miles the highway was close on the bank of a pretty river called the Muskingum, and with tall hills and green farms on every side it was something to remember.

That afternoon we crossed the Ohio River again into West Virginia at a small place near Allegheny mountains, but as it was foggy and rainy the whole time we missed a lot of the scenery.

In Virginia we saw some very interesting small towns with old, old colonial houses and all of them with a Revolutionary background. We had a fine lunch at a café in Winchester, where George Washington was supposed to have spent much time.

About 2 pm Tuesday we arrived the home of Matt's sister who lives with her 16 year old son Dick on a farm about 9 miles from Alexandria, Va and about 12 miles from Washington D. C. Harry was tired and went to bed immediately but Kathie took the car and drove us through Alexandria and Washington. We could write a whole letter about Alexandria alone, but of course Washington was the high spot.

Going through Alexandria we saw the Masonic Memorial to Geo.

Washington. This was a graceful white marble structure covering a large area and towering as high as a twenty story building you can see for miles. Almost all the houses in Alexandria date back to the Revolutionary War, or even farther. They are certainly picturesque and make you feel that you are almost living in Colonial times. About 5 miles from there we crossed the Potomac River into Washington. There is really too much to see at this point. There is Arlington Cemetery, the Bridge,—Bird Sanctuaries and Washington itself. We could see the Washington Monument and the Capital Dome from the Memorial Bridge in spite of rain and fog. We drove through all the main avenues, seeing all sides of the Capitol, the White House the Lincoln Memorial, Library of Congress, Treasury and all the principal government buildings and landmarks. We also saw the main shopping section and ran into some real big city traffic when thousands of government employees started home for the night. We drove far out on Hayn's Point on the Potomac where they have anchored every kind of pleasure boat from a skiff to a yacht. Finally we went to the Washington Air Port, and saw a huge transport plane leave for Chicago.

We left Virginia early Wednesday morning after spending the night at Kathie's. We passed through Washington again, but it was still pouring rain and kept on pouring until we reached Baltimore, Md. about 9:30 am. We did not see the down-town section there, but plenty of other interesting sights. This was the most unusual town we saw. There was block after block of brick houses of all colors. The houses in each block are identical and are built one into the next with no yard between. Each and every apartment in these blocks has its white front steps which are kept white and spotless, the women trying to outdo each other in this detail all the time, no matter how the rest of the house looks. This actually continues for miles as you drive along, and there is an air of colonial quaintness that you find nowhere else, all the inns and roadhouses pattern themselves along the same line and try to identify themselves with some historic person or event. Shortly after this we passed into Pennsylvania and drove for many miles thru beautiful scenery and interesting towns. We passed an immense dam (or rather the road crossed the river on it) on the Susquehanna River that furnishes power for the whole Pennsylvania Railroad. As we neared

Philadelphia, Louise and I thought we were in the city miles before we actually reached it. The highway became broad enough for 6 cars to pass comfortably and beautiful estates and parks on every side. We never got near the business section and there was too much fog to see the skyline, but, as in Baltimore there was plenty to see in the outskirts. It took us about an hour to pass thru these suburbs, seeing all sorts of Universities, parks, factories, and an enormous mail-order branch of Sears Roebuck. (We saw a similar one of Montgomery Ward's at Baltimore). As we were leaving Philadelphia, we drove for 12 miles through a park lined by rows of beautiful homes and apartments on each side. The road was doubled with a boulevard in the center and room for 3 cars abreast on each side. This is really part of the Lincoln Highway which we traveled all the way from Washington to N. Y. C.. The 98 miles between Philadelphia and New York were the most interesting part of the trip. This road was 6 lanes wide all the way in. It is as smooth as a table and runs almost perfectly straight the whole distance. We passed about a mile from Princeton, N. J. and could plainly see the towers of the university buildings. We crossed the Delaware River at Trenton, N. J. By the time we neared Newark the traffic became really thick on the highway and everybody moved at a fast pace. We saw several who had been stopped by state troopers—not to mention ourselves. As we passed thru Newark we saw the largest and busiest airport in the U. S. A. We saw at least 12 large transport planes taking off or lying in wait. This is a large town (Newark) but Jersey City is much more so, in fact we thought it was part of New York. As we passed through here we saw so many factories, buildings and houses, it would be impossible to describe them. The traffic here was surely something to see—cars from every state. We passed and were passed several times by a family of wild-looking gypsies in a huge old Buick with a Mississippi license. They drove rather recklessly in and out of traffic for a long way, but you should have seen them simmer down when a trooper appeared on the road. We had an interesting experience passing under the Hudson River. As we entered the tunnel there were two policemen standing there taking the 50 cent fee just as fast as they could reach out. Harry says they do that all day and night, the traffic thru the tunnel is so heavy. Cars in the tunnel

121

must stay 75 feet apart and are not allowed to blow their horns (the noise would be deafening). When we came out on Manhattan we were right in the busiest part of New York. There were numberless tall buildings and the first familiar object we saw was the Woolworth Tower and a few minutes later we recognized the Chrysler and Empire State Buildings. Before we crossed the Island we drove along the docks on the Hudson River, and saw several of the largest ocean liners afloat. The Europa, the Ile-de-France and Alimited Fruit-South American liner. This last was the most beautiful of all. We reached the other side of the Island after traveling through places that were awe-inspiring—at least to us!

We crossed East River on the Queensborough Bridge which passes over Welfare Island. We could see the skyline towering behind us and in a few minutes were on Long Island and home.

Well, if you have got this far I guess you are ready to quit. The next letter we will try to tell you something of what we have seen here in New York.

We sure do miss you and would be mighty homesick if there was time to
think about it. But Harry and Matt have certainly made us comfortable and welcome.

We want to hear from you as soon as possible.

Love from H. B., Louise and Pat

P.S. The package arrived here o.k. the day
before we did.

August 31, 1937

Dear Mom, Dad and Kids,

   We were sure glad to get your letters and to hear that you are all o.k. Tell Dick he would really see some sail boats if he were to come up to Jamaica Bay on the south shore of Long Island. We passed there Sunday afternoon on our way to Rock-Away Beach in the same section. This bay is more like a group of salt lakes extending inland for several miles. We rode over them to the ocean on a long concrete bridge, Hundreds of people were fishing from this bridge and seemed to be doing pretty well.
   At Rockaway Beach we saw the ocean for the first time and was that a thrill. The day was marred by heavy clouds and fog which have persisted ever since we came here, but the scenery was grand, nevertheless. The ocean was gray-blue with enormous breakers rolling up the sand and over the bathers who numbered into the hundreds of thousands as far in each direction as we could see. At one time we counted 19 airplanes circling overhead, some of them towing great advertising signs which appeared to be at least a block long. We saw hundreds of beautiful summer homes on Long Island, and in this section people roam the streets in bathing suits and every kind of nondescript clothing in perfect ease.
   Louise and I have already been to town several times. We have seen so much it is hard to know where to start. Anyway I went down with Jack and Billy Wednesday night. Jack had to sell papers and Billy and I walked along the streets window shopping. We went over to the world famous Times Square and by night this is the most unbelievable place one could think of. The whole place is ablaze with lights of every color. The buildings seem to have no top, losing themselves in the night. Along the streets the shop windows are dressed and lit up to fit the brilliance of the whole scene and there is nothing one can think of that cannot be seen displayed in these windows. The evidence of wealth and lavish expense shows in

everything you see, and these stores go to any end to outdo each other in attracting the public. The same is to be said of the theatrical section on Broadway and 42nd Street just off Times Square. I saw all the big theatres I read and studied so much about in my sign books. Some of their lobbies are really art museums with elaborate paintings and displays of scenes from their programs. Thursday morning, Billy, Bobby and I went to the Roxy (25 cents till 1 o'clock) saw a long screen program which combined with a stage show lasted 3 ½ hours. This theatre seems more like a palace and in its different lobbies and corridors they have displayed some world famous paintings and art works.

We go from Harry's house to Manhattan by subway (you can ride all day for 5 cents) going under the East River and coming up in Grand Central Station or several Street Entrances such as 5th Avenue or Times Square. If we go to town in the car we cross East River on the Queensborough Bridge, getting a magnificent view of the skyline. It is about 3 miles from Harry's house to Times Square and from his front porch we can see the Empire State Building, Radio City and other big buildings. Friday afternoon we spent some time in Macy's store. This place is better than a Sears Roebuck catalog come to life. It covers an entire city block and has 12 complete floors open to the public. Their toy department occupys half of one floor and it is a high spot of interest to people of every age. They have everything from building blocks to small automobiles with real motors. If Dick could see their Boating and Sports Dept. he would never go back to Paducah. You can buy anything from a canoe to a small sloop, completely equipped. All other departments are just as complete and I believe you could spend a week in that store alone without seeing everything. I have my application in there for work in their art department, but have not been able to see the right man yet. I had an interview with the display manager at Gimbel's another huge store about the size of Macy's. He said he had hired a man about an hour before I came in but that he would give me a try if this man did not meet his expectations. I tried another big store—Saks 5th Avenue—they were very nice and took my application, but do not have such a large art department. We also left applications at several employment agencies and it is with them that we have the most hope. I want to

see several other places today if I can get around fast enough. It
takes all day long to get from place to place and to find the right
party to talk to. You can't understand how large New York really is
until you try to get around in it on foot. One does not get tired so
quickly, however, because there is always something new to see.
One of the most amusing things to see on the streets is the large
number of foreigners peddling fake merchandise like 25 cent wrist
watches and toy dogs that appear to bark (but do not, as the
peddlers are ventriloquists). Others sell blow up balloons. The one
they show is very like a dirigible and several feet long, but the one
they give you proves to be very small and no account. Others want
to take your picture, sell song books, needle threaders and
everything else. I guess they consider all suckers to be fair game, but
we have not been taken in by any of them yet. These fellows peddle
illegally and have to pick up there stands and scoot for the next
block when they see a cop.

But it would take a book to tell what we have seen downtown
and we have only scratched the surface as yet.

Saturday night we drove into Astoria (northwest of Woodside on
Long Island.) This place is larger than Louisville, has an enormous
business section, but there is no apparent division between it and
the rest of New York of which it is a part. Here we saw and close
hand the famous Hell Gate and Triborough Bridges which connect
Astoria and Queens with the Bronx and Manhattan. By night
and brilliantly lighted the Triborough was beautiful and fantastic
in the extreme with a continual stream of cars passing hundreds of
feet above where we parked. Hell gate is a railroad bridge and was
dark and shadowy but a more graceful structure than the
Triborough. Here we saw several large boats bucking the tidal
eddies, a meeting of rough and dangerous currents caused by the
tide rising and meeting itself coming from New York Harbor up
East River and meeting the same rise coming from Long Island
Sound. We saw a beautiful power yacht heading out into the
Sound with a lot of rich people on a weekend party. They had an
orchestra aboard and were making plenty of noise. Harry says those
outings of the rich get plenty rowdy in the late hours.

Well, I'll have to turn this over to Louise and she will tell you
more. No, she says she is so exhausted from our all day walk, she

will have to write a separate letter later. Before I close I must say that we got our biggest thrill yet out of Central Station, a city in itself. The ceiling of the Grand Lobby is several stories above the floor and occupies an enormous space. Leading off on every side are corridors which are more like streets with beautiful stores on every side and there are several levels of these underground. You can buy almost anything imaginable without ever leaving the station. Here you can see people of every race and nationality going about there work or saying goodbye to friends as they leave for different parts of the world.

Well, in spite of this interesting city, we must say we miss you all and all the things we were used to and are becoming a little homesick. The large percentage of foreigners and strange people on every hand make this place a hard one to like and we feel a little hesitant even now about trying to settle here. People here seem to care absolutely nothing about making friends or helping each other out. At places I have applied for work they are rather cold and unoblidging. Well, it all depends on what kind of job I can land. I will have to do much better than in Paducah to want to stay here. Matt and Harry and all the others have certainly been nice and have helped us as much as they could. Well, write soon and we will do the same.

Patsy wants to write a postscript.

> *Love to all,*
> *H. B., Louise and Patsy*

She says hello.

September 4, 1937

Dearest Folks,

Started a letter to you last nite but it was late and I was so sleepy decided I had better wait until today.

We are really having some hot weather up here, it is equal to what we have in Paducah, everyone says it is very unusual, however there is always a wonderful breeze through Matt's living room, the house sits right in the middle of a street and nothing to obstruct the air. The view from her windows is very pretty especially when it is a clear day and you can see the skyline.

H.B.and I had planned to go uptown to the Roxy Theatre last nite but company came so the boys, H.B.and Harry went out by themselves to see pictures of the prize fight.

Miss Helen Moreland, the radio announcer came out and had supper with us last nite, she has just returned from her vacation in Calif. made the trip in 17 hrs. said it was lovely, a wonderful trip and that on board they can't seem to do enough for your comfort.

Matt and Harry, Dorothy and another couple drove over to N. J. to meet the plane and missed it as it arrived two hours ahead. So the couple a Mr and Mrs. Schnable took them up to their penthouse apt. Dorothy said it was lovely but there was just too much height. They have their terrace flowers, plants and even trees.

Last Sat. afternoon H.B.Pat Bill and I went out to Central park Zoo. Patsy didn't seem to care a great deal about it but I believe I could spend a whole day there. It is a beautiful place, lakes all through, swans, ducks, etc, even two huge pelicans and they come right up to be fed. That isn't the big Zoo however it seemed pretty big to us.

We took some pictures but haven't had them developed as yet.

Mary Lee we certainly enjoyed your letter and hope you will write another real soon. Patsy made me read it to her and this morning ask for it again, she says she is going to write you all real soon.

The boys really keep her in hot water. Bobby would rather tease her than eat—she fusses with them and of course that is just what

127

they want.

We are all planning on going out to Rockaway beach this afternoon. We were out there last Sunday but didn't go in, they really have a mob out there it was pretty warm going out but we were only out there few minutes when we began to cool off and believe me before we left there we were nearly frozen. The ocean makes an awful noise roaring. People seem to have a good time riding the waves. While out there we saw several big liners off quite a distance.

We were anxious to go on board a big ship but they want $1.00 just to go through the Normandy so we decided to pass that up as there are so many other places to go and see.

I haven't as yet been near Radio City or Empire State bldg. H.B.has and you should see how he gets about by himself in this place. The subway is quite an experience, we are only about twenty minutes from Times Sq. catch a sub. just couple blocks from here and go under the river come up in Grand Central Station the very minute you hit the tubes leading under water your ears nearly burst. It positively terrified me the first trip we made. They go like lightening and you can think a million things, however I am more used to it now.

Wish you could all see the stores, they are almost fairyland there is a big "Kress"store on Fifth Ave and it nearly takes you breath, doesn't' even look like a 5 &10.

Macy's is beautiful we as yet have only go on five floors and even then didn't see everything on each floor. All the big stores are air conditioned. Another pretty store "Gimble's" luxury in itself and when you enter from the hot street it is so cool and there is a heavenly scent either sachet or perfume all over the main floor, beautiful and yet not so very expensive.

Sak's Fifth Ave. is really something as Dad say's it costs you five dollars to get past the front entrance. The stores are to lovely for words. Lavish displays of every description seems that money is as free as water where it comes to decorating the stores.

The one big drawback to this place is that it simply takes forever to go any place, of course if you know your way about it doesn't take so long but one of their blocks would equal two or three of ours.

If you go shopping seems you just can't possibly go through more than two or three stores.

We have only taken Pat down once to see toyland at "Macy's" as it is really hard on all of us, her little legs give out in no time. H.B.said he never saw such big children riding around in baby buggies and that is true but it is because of such distance also hills, this is a very hilly place.

N. Y. is a true melting pot. I never dreamed there were so many foreigners in the whole U. S. It is with relief when you finally run into someone who speaks as you do. You can't make heads or tails of what they are saying.

This is a great place for visiting and sightseeing but we are not so sure of it for living. You don't find nice little cottages like you do many places, nearly everything is either apts. or two family houses such as Mat's. Harry says there are sections out around N. Y. but the houses rent from $50, $60, $90 a mo.

H.B.has just come in from town so will turn this over to him. Write real soon tell Louise we would like to hear from them give our regards to McClures, Leighs, Emerys.

Love to all,
Louise

Dear Folks —-

*Louise has told you about a lot of the places we have visited to-
gether, and I would like to tell you of some of the things I have seen
myself while walking these streets looking for a job. I have aver-
aged going to Manhattan twice a day all this week, spending practically all day in town, seeing or trying to see people who might do
me some good. Consequently, I have not been able to pay much attention to sight-seeing. I have registered at about 12 big employment agencies, and as these have been widely separated, it has
taken nearly all week to see them and the department stores I have
tried. It really takes hours here to go anywhere here, even by bus or
subway. The thermometer has stayed close to 100 –degrees here all
week, and I have had to wear my suit the whole time. No one here
goes coatless even in the hottest weather—that is—in the downtown section. Experienced help here in New York are paid much
less than outsiders are led to believe. Few besides professional people
make more than 35.00 wk. And the big majority do not get even
that much. Ordinary firms pay their window trimmers and card
writers about 25.00 wk.*

*Stores like Macy's, Gimbels, Saks 5th Ave, Bloomingdales, Lud-
wig Berman, Etc pay some better. And it is with them that we
have the most hope, as they have talked very favorably to me.*

*However we are becoming less enthusiastic about New York as a
place to live, every day we are here. There is plenty here to see and
do, if you have a good income and a means to get about. Of course,
if we had a well-paid job up here it would make us feel differently.*

*But unless I do get a job in the display dept. of a big store, I guess
we will be back before long.*

*These independent sign shops, and studios bitterly resent an out of
town artist trying to locate here, and do everything they can to
make it impossible.*

*Thursday I had interviews with some advertising executives who
hold really big jobs and have plenty of influence up here. They talk
very encouragingly to me about my work though of course they said*

I was unqualified to hold a job as commercial artist. They advised me to get into one of the big stores, as the rest of the signs and theatre art jobs are completely in the hands of crooked unions.

One of these fellows was Mr. Paul G. Trimble, advertising manager of H. Donnelly Co., a firm that publishes everything from magazines to telephone books and occupy about 12 floors in a big skyscraper here. I was recommended and sent to him by a friend of Harry's who knows him well. He (Trimble) is the most human, understanding fellow I ever talked to. Although I was a perfect stranger to him, he immediately started trying to locate a place for me, calling several of his friends and telling them to keep a lookout for a job for me. He talked to me about an hour about my work and my future (if any) in N. Y. I am to see him again next week.

Then I went to an advertising agency on 5th Avenue. Mr. Trimble knew them well and called them before I left his office. This firm was a prosperous organization of artists and advertising men—Kelsey, Buanni and DeBellis—

I talked to the first two fellows a long time. They were as kind and considerate as Mr. Trimble, advising me how to go about seeing the right people to help me get along up here. Even at that it is certainly confusing trying to "see somebody" in this immense place. I suppose though that I will know within a week or two about what our chances are up here.

Well, I guess that is about enough to say about our personal experiences up here.

This afternoon about 1:30 we all got in the car and started across Long Island for Jones Beach, which is an internationally famous bathing resort and open free of charge to the public (it is really a state park.)

Jones Beach is also on the south shore of Long Island, but further east than Rockaway, being about 50 miles from New York City. Don't let anyone tell you that Long Island is a small place! Although it looks like a pin point on the map, it is really 140 miles long and about 50 wide. During the drive to the beach we saw some of the most beautiful, densely wooded country I have ever seen in my life. The west end of the island and the parts bordering the ocean are densely populated, but the interior has some really wild country interrupted by rich estates, big airports, polo fields, racetracks and green farms. All the principal highways out of New York into Long Island are really 4 roads in one, running side by side, but spacious as they are, they barely take care of the heavy traffic, and even in the open country there are plenty of policemen and stop lights. One feature seen on highways in that part of the country that is unknown in Kentucky are the enormous roadside markets which sell every kind of fruit and vegetable known and numerous other things from orange marmalade (homemade) and blueberry pie to apple and cherry (!) cider. They make brilliant displays and really stand out against the green countryside Anyway, we arrived at Jones Beach about 2:30. We paid 25 cents at a toll bridge on the way and a 25 cent parking charge for the car at the beach and that was all the outing cost the bunch of us. They have several solidly paved parking lots at this one beach, in all capable of handling 10,000 cars. And on a hot day traffic has to be turned away.

Before we reached the beach we passed miles of salt water lakes and bays covered with expensive pleasure boats. One of the larger bays contained an enormous floating stage anchored about 100 yds from the shore. On this musical comedies and light operas are given every nite of the summer season.

The audience is seated on a semicircular stadium on the shore, and they say the stage spectacle viewed from there is really wonder-ful. You can attend these performances for as little as 25 cents. The show playing now is "The Circus Princess."

All the bathhouses and other buildings at Jones Beach are of beautiful brick and stone structures. And the whole place is landscaped with gardens and interwinding lawns and pavements which conceal the ocean until you step out onto the beach. This beach is about 100 yards wide and the sand is perfectly clean and dazzling white. Combining this scene with a deep blue ocean, bright colored beach umbrellas and thousands of people in every kind of costume, you have a scene not to be equaled anywhere.

And it was a thrill to actually go into the ocean and ride in on white breakers, many of which were way over our heads, but quite harmless. Time went by in a hurry this way, and from time to time we would stop and dig in the wet sand for tiny fiddler crabs—

about the size of a peach seed and colored white and speckled gray. These must live in the sand by countless millions as you actually cannot scoop your hand into the wet sand without picking up one or more of them, but they will scuttle for the water at a terrific rate and bury themselves in the ooze so quick you can't see how it's done.

Needless to say this and our other trip to the ocean are just about the crowning experience of our lives and we sure wish you could enjoy them with us. If we should decide to settle up here, we will never rest until you all can come up here and see some of these wonderful things.

Oh, yes, while at the beach, we saw a four-masted sailing vessel so far away it was half-hidden over the horizon. Also a big liner!

Well, we have hardly seen anything yet, want to visit Battery Park Aquarium, the Metropolitan Museum of Art, the Museum of Natural History, the Bronx Zoo and numerous other things.

We are beginning to learn a few of the down-town streets and subway routes which seemed hopelessly complicated at first. We still get a kick out of riding them. They go like the wind (subway trains) and have 12 or 15 coaches which are always crowded whether at noon or two o'clock in the morning. We seldom go to Manhattan except by subway under the East River (you can always tell when the train is under the river by increased pressure on the eardrums). Almost all seasoned subway riders have their noses in a newspaper, seldom saying anything or looking up, but miraculously do, just in time to get off at the right station, which may be three floors above or 3 below ground. These trains follow each other in such rapid succession, we never have to wait more than two or three minutes no matter where we are.

Well, in closing, we never see enough to keep us from missing you all. Write us soon. I guess we will know in a few days what we are going to do.

Love to all
Louise, H.B.and Pat

Sept. 12, 1937

Dear Mom, Dad and Kids:

We can't remember who owes who a letter, but we have seen so many interesting things the last few days, we have material enough for several letters.

I had a pretty tough week this last one. Miles and miles of walking and subway riding, and very little success. I suppose I could have been working before this, if I had been willing to take a low paid job, but there would be no sense in that, as we are still "unsold" on New York as a place to live. Friday I was asked to report at the art department of Arnold Constable's, a big department store on 5th Avenue.

They had virtually promised me a week's work writing cards for a special sale, but when I reported, they said they had changed their minds and that their regular man could handle it by himself. The next day I went back to Gimble's and they told me to be on hand Wednesday morning (Sept. 15) to go to work in the sign department. We are dubious about this job, for I do not think it will pay much and they give no assurance that it will be regular.

Maybe it will be good experience though, if just for a few days. Unless this turns out to be a very good job, I expect we will start home in about a week, for the more we see of New York, the less we want to stay here.

Friday nite, Louise and I went to a double-feature show at the Harris Theatre on Times Square; for only 20 cents we saw Dick Powell in "The Singing Marine" and John Beel in "The Man Who Found Himself" which was really the best. Last Tuesday we went to the Roxy and for 25 cents saw a big time stage show and a complete screen program featuring Sonja Heine in "Thin Ice".

Tell J. B. that we saw Ruth Aarons, world champion table tennis player in an exhibition match on the stage of the Roxy. She played against a young man who is the English champion. That game is very popular up here and most of the billiard halls and amusement palaces have tables where people play for a small fee.

Monday, Labor Day, we all went out to the Bronx Park which is a beautiful wooded tract covering a very large area. The Bronx is across the Harlem River from Manhattan, to the north, and is the cities largest Jewish section. They live there in crowded apartments by the hundreds of thousands. Some of these apartment houses are beautiful to behold, many of them modernistic and built of every color of tile and brick. Streets lined with these really continue for miles. Many of the stores in this section are designated with Hebrew signs with just a word or two of English —the population in this section is so largely Jewish. We also saw many Jews of a poorer type coming through Harlem. This was undoubtedly the dirtiest smelliest, the most crowded place we have ever seen. Poor classes of every nationality live here, with every race and color living together in the same apartments. The streets are alive with kids of every description, skating, flying kites, shooting craps and fighting, all the while dodging heavy traffic. They have no other place to play. Before we reached Harlem we drove for many blocks along Park Avenue, the most expensive and exclusive residential district to be found anywhere. But here, as everywhere else in New York, there are only apartment houses, many of them skyscrapers. (We have not seen a single-family dwelling in New York —any part of the city). No house seems to hold less than two families, and there are few like that. Anyway Park Avenue is alive with big shiny cars and snooty looking people, and every

apartment has its uniformed flunky standing at the front entrance.

But to get back to the Bronx Zoo; it is supposed to be one of the world's largest, and we did see a lot of interesting things, but the park is so large, we were too tired to see nearly all of it.

The exhibits are widely scattered, and we would have had to walk many miles to see it all. The walks and roadways are closely crowded by enormous trees and heavy undergrowth. It is really wild and there are lakes and streams where hundreds of wild ducks and geese stay all the time. You see many beautiful varieties there, all protected by law. One building there contains the largest collection of mounted game specimens in the world. Also, guns and weapons used by famous hunters from Daniel Boone on down. We all thought this to be the most interesting thing in the Park. A disagreeable, but ever-present feature of attending the public amusement spots is the crowds which swarm everywhere and through which you have to push if you expect to see anything. This place is so big that no matter whether

135

you go to a show, a park or just to town, there is always a crowd ahead of you, about 5% of them speaking real American.

Anyway we came home about 3:30 having spent about 4 hours in the Park. This time we came over the Triborough Bridge which connects Long Island, Manhattan and the Bronx. This bridge is very high and we got a grand view of all three sections, especially that Manhattan skyline. I do not know how far the Bronx Park is from Harry's house, but the latter is on 53rd St. Long Island and the park starts at 180th Street in the Bronx. We saw a bus labeled "242 St and White Plains Ave." just to give you some idea of how far you have to go up here to see anything. But it was an interesting day.

Saturday afternoon, Louise and I intended to visit the Museum of Natural History, but as it closes early, we decided on Battery Park. We went by subway to Times Square, and changed to a "downtown" local train. Getting off at Battery Park we were right on New York harbor with East River on the left and the Hudson on the right. The first thing we saw was the Statue of Liberty on Bedloe Island, and it is certainly the outstanding landmark in the harbor, even though a couple of miles distant. To add to the thrill of seeing it there was a German freighter steaming out past it to the sea. It was a beautiful sight, even though the "swastika" was on her funnels. The harbor was alive with boats and we could also see Ellis Island and the Jersey Coast. All this kept us occupied for some time and then we went to the Aquarium which is close at hand in Battery Park. After going through this we both agreed it was the most interesting place to visit in all New York. It is a very large circular building on the site of an old fort used to guard the harbor in Colonial times. Once inside (it's entirely free—this whole outing cost us only 20 cents—subway fare) we were confronted with two tiers of beautifully lighted glass tanks going all the way around the inside of the building. We start at the right, going upstairs and around a circular walk that follows the upper row of tanks. We saw every variety fresh water and sea fish imaginable, sea horses, starfish, shellfish, crabs, lobsters and fish—from large sharks in immense tanks down to bright tropical fish no larger than your fingernail. We saw 8-foot electric eels that have enough power to knock down a horse, at least the sign said so. And when they discharge electricity a light turns on in front of their tank.

The tanks containing fish are so arranged that it is just like looking into store windows and inside are cleverly made to look like a glimpse into the ocean. The tanks contain rocks, coral and plants to which the fish are accustomed in their natural home. The larger fish, such as sharks and the big eels are on the lower level.

Enclosed in this circular wall of tanks are several larger ones open at the top. These are filled with live penguins and sea birds, turtles, alligators, etc. One could spend many hours in this place without tiring. The ceiling and border have been beautifully painted with undersea scenes to further the submarine atmosphere of this place. We would give anything if you all could have had this outing.

When we went back we stopped downtown or rather uptown and did some shopping in the Kress 10 cent store on 5th Aveue. This is the best one in New York, covering over half a block, with a street floor and two basements. It is a beautiful modernistic building of white stone. It is just as beautiful inside, really the finest in this big city. Walls and ceiling are covered with intricate carved and relief work. The ceiling is almost lacy with openings for the indirect lighting and air conditioning systems. The floors are paved with blocks of some marble veined plastic which is noiseless and easy on tired feet. This store contains the biggest variety of desirable and beautiful things we have ever seen. Some of the more notable departments are the toy and novelty sections. There is a large department containing nothing but pure white pottery. In the first basement there is an artificial flower department (no crepe paper, either) running the whole length of the store. It is really dazzling, and on the other side a store-length jewelry counter. It is very hard to leave this really colorful and pleasant store ——just about the most restful place we have been in ——due to the air-conditioning and soft lighting and you could stay in there all day and not see everything.

This store even has two separate cafeterias. There is a Woolworth store nearby that has more floor space, but it is not nearly so fine and does not seem to have the variety of beautiful things to be found in the Kress store. There seems to be any number of 5 and 10 companies up here, but we have not seen a Kresge store yet. There are several Sears Roebuck stores up here and a very large Montgomery Ward store in Jamaica, Long Island near here.

Well, we wrote the above last night and now it is Monday, very cold and pouring rain. There have been several times lately when an overcoat would have helped. As a whole the weather has been pretty since we came up here, but changes very suddenly. Last Saturday when we went to Jones Beach it was perfectly clear and almost before we got home, there was one of the most violent thunderstorms we have ever seen. The weather has seemed like fall ever since and this morning is uncomfortably cool. The boys are starting to school today. The school which Billy attends has 9,000 students, and operates in shifts. Billy does not go until 11 o'clock in the morning, and stays till nearly 6 pm. This school has 600 different classes a day.

Yesterday, Louise and I left about 12 o'clock and started for the American Museum of Natural History. We are learning the subway and elevated lines a little better and are not so scared to go places by ourselves. The museum is at 79th Street and Central Park West— quite a distance from Harry's. It is in a small park of its own, and the Hayden Planetarium is on the same grounds opening into the museum. They have two daily lectures during which the skys are projected on a great dome-shaped ceiling that is startlingly real. They have real meteorites and celestial bodies on display here. And beautiful pictures on glass of stars and planets, beautifully lighted from behind.

We spent about 3 hours in the museum itself and saw some of the principal things of interest, but it would take days to get all over it. To me, the African Room was the most outstanding place there and you enter it first from the front. This room contains the three exhibits pictured in Life Magazine several weeks ago. The one with the zebras and giraffe at the water hole is the first one you see on entering. If it is possible to make a choice this is the finest single exhibit in the room. It contains more different animals in poses so real it is hard to believe they are dead. The earth, rocks and plants are artificial, but perfect replicas of the real things, made at tremendous cost. The backgrounds of mountains, forests, and sky are clev-

erly painted on curved settings, that certainly look like the out of doors. They were painted by fine artists and the illusion of sunlight and shade and distance is so perfect, one can scarcely tell where the painting stops and the real trees and plants begin.

There are about 15 of these exhibits in the African room alone, hermetically sealed behind glass, bigger than any store windows in Paducah.

The gorilla scene is especially effective. Through thick "jungle" growth you can see distant purple mountains partly hidden by real looking clouds.

In the Asiatic room, one of the cases showed a large red deer, attacked by a pack of wild dogs. They were circled about the deer in dramatic action poses. There was even one lying dead at the deers feet.

There was a mud-hole behind the deer (it really looked like fresh mud and has for years). Some of the dogs had muddy legs and the deer was bespattered. Even the rocks and grass were spotted with mud kicked up in the "fight."

Some of the displays showed animals and birds drinking from forest pools which were of glass, but were perfectly real, even to ripples and bubbles caused by the drinking animal. We saw the illusion of water brought to perfection in the fish room where fish and even small whales are shown in underwater settings.

Louise was most taken with the mineral room. This contains thousands of mineral curiosities and enormously valuable jewels in their natural state. There are also many cases filled with antique jewelry of gold, agate and jade. They show cross sections of fossil tree trunks that are purer agate.

In the prehistoric room we saw the worlds greatest collection of dinosaur skeletons, many of them complete. The walls and ceiling of this room were covered with beautiful paintings of prehistoric scenes. Another room contained many original paintings by Audubon, as well as many of his personal belongings.

Well, we cannot tell you a tenth of the things we saw, and this also was entirely free, except for the lectures in the planetarium which we passed up, being able to see a lot of it from the entrance.

I guess you all think we are painting these things in glowing terms, but even at that we can't show you how interesting they re-

ally are. We could come back to Paducah satisfied if you all could see them too. If we have gone into too much detail, excuse us, and we will talk of more personal things when we come back. In spite of all we have seen, we still want to go home, unless this job at Gimbles' turns out to be very good.

Well, let us hear from you, and we'll tell you very soon about when we are coming back.

Love to all ,
H. B., Louise and Patsy

The great adventure ended with our coming back to Paducah by Greyhound Bus on September 19, 1937. When we returned home, my father received word of a firm job offer at Arnold Constable. However, he was firm in his conviction that New York City was no place for us to live and he returned to his job as lobby artist for the Columbia Amusement Company.

My younger brother, Paul, joined us on June 1, 1941 and my father continued to work in that little sign shop at the Arcade until he took a wartime job at a defense plant, Kentucky Ordinance Works in 1943. That job ended on V-J Day, August 14, 1945.

After the job at K. O. W. ended, he returned to the sign shop in the Arcade Theatre building. In the late 1940's, movie advertising methods began to change. The big lobby signs were not used as much anymore. Television would soon begin to have a serious effect on movie attendance. Although he continued to do the smaller jobs the theatres now needed, he went to work at Sanders-Troutman Sign Shop, then opened his own sign shop at 1214 Broadway. When Union Carbide built its plant near Paducah, he went to work in the sign shop and worked there until his retirement in 1974. After his retirement, he continued his commercial art work in a shop in his garage and developed a skill in calligraphy that, in addition to his art and sign work, gave him a steady business and great personal satisfaction.

The most important aspect of the lives of both my parents, however, was their abiding faith in God. They were dedicated Christians, and my father served as deacon at First Baptist Church of Paducah and as teacher of the Adult Men's Bible Class. My mother taught Sunday School in the Primary Department for many years. They were married for sixty-two years and they lived their faith each day.

How blessed I was to have them.

Rivergees

Bibliography

Paducah's Super Flood, by Fred G. Neuman

My Paducah, by Barron White

Paducah City Directory, 1936

The Paducah Sun-Democrat, January, 1937

Rivergees